Enduring war and health inquality in Sri Lanka

978-1-85201-021-8

Published by:
Tamil Information Centre (TIC)
Thulasi
Bridge End Close (off Clifton Road)
Kingston-upon-Thames KT2 6PZ
United Kingdom

Tel: + 44 (0)20 8546 1560
Fax: + 44 (0)20 8546 5701
E-mail: info.tic@sangu.org
Website: www.tamilinfo.org

Authors:
Mayan Vije
Dr Suppiah Ratneswaren

Editorial advisors:
Marion Birch
Professor Jane Salvage

ENDURING WAR AND HEALTH INEQUALITY
IN SRI LANKA

Mayan Vije
Suppiah Ratneswaren

A Publication of Tamil Information Centre, UK

Contents

Figures

Tables

Graphs

Maps

Boxes

1: Repeated failures to make peace, 1985-2008
2: The Oslo Declaration, 2002
3: Threats to children's rights and well-being
4: Essential elements of the right to health
5: Children killed by air force bombing
6: Government restrictions on materials to northern Sri Lanka, 2001
7: Violations of human rights and humanitarian law
8: Trends in crop production
9: UN condemns torture in Sri Lanka
10: A mother sees her son lose his arm
11: Regional disparities
12: Criticisms of government health information
13: No shelter from the monsoon
14: Snakebite deaths in a village
15: Nothing obscured the suffering

Abbreviations

AI	Amnesty International
ADB	Asian Development Bank
AHRC	Asian Human Rights Commission
BRC	British Refugee Council
CHA	Consortium of Humanitarian Agencies
CPA	Centre for Policy Alternatives
ER	Emergency Regulations
EU	European Union
FAO	Food and Agricultural Organization
FIAN	Foodfirst Information and Action Network International
FMM	Free Media Movement
GDP	Gross Domestic Product
HRW	Human Rights Watch
ICRC	International Committee of the Red Cross
IDP	Internally displaced persons
IDMC	Internal Displacement Monitoring Centre
IFSP	Integrated Food Security Programme
IIGEP	International Independent Group of Eminent Persons
IPCS	Institute of Peace and Conflict Studies
IRIN	Integrated Regional Information Network
JVP	Janatha Vimukthi Peramuna (People's Liberation Front)
LKR	Sri Lanka rupees
L & ST	Law and Society Trust
LTTE	Liberation Tigers of Tamil Eelam
MSF	Médecins sans Frontières
NGO	Nongovernmental organization
OHCHR	Office of the High Commissioner for Human Rights
PTA	Prevention of Terrorism Act
P-TOMS	Post-Tsunami Operational Management System
SLG	Sri Lanka Government
SLMM	Sri Lanka Monitoring Mission
TIC	Tamil Information Centre
TMVP	Tamil Makkal Viduthalai Pulikal (Tamil People's Liberation Tigers)
UN	United Nations
UNDP	UN Development Programme
UNHCR	UN High Commissioner for Refugees
UNHRC	UN Human Rights Council
UNICEF	UN Children's Fund
UN OCHA	UN Office for the Coordination of Humanitarian Affairs
WFP	World Food Programme
WHO	World Health Organization

Acknowledgements

Tamil Information Centre (TIC) is grateful to several individuals in Sri Lanka and around the world who have shared information and contributed to this report, and must remain anonymous for security reasons.

TIC expresses its sincere thanks to Marion Birch at Medact for her advice and support, and Jane Salvage for her editorial assistance. Special mention must be made of Varadakumar and Dr N Sivarajah for being excellent sources of information and their continued support. Richard Rathwell and Patrick Dennis are thanked for their constructive comments of the manuscript. Anenta's great help every step of the way and her contribution to this project deserve special mention.

Preface

During the preparation of this report we were confronted by several information barriers including a scarcity of reliable sources, a lack of systematic collection of data on war-related morbidity and mortality, a lack of comparative data for regions within Sri Lanka, and limited publications on the health consequences of this war. The Sri Lankan Annual Health Bulletins, produced by the Ministry of Health, do not address these aspects and very often exclude data from the North-East region.

Since preparing this report the situation has worsened with conflict escalating between the Sri Lankan government and the LTTE. According to the latest reports, 250,000 people have been trapped in a pocket in Vanni. All international NGOs have been asked to leave by the government and there is no independent media to report or verify the situation.

Food and medicine have been restricted from LTTE areas. Several hospitals have been destroyed by repeated attacks and patients are being treated in temporary makeshift shelters. Eight doctors with no specialist skills are having to cope with unmanageable demands. Patients that have been transferred to hospitals under government military control are subjected to restricted access to their families.

According to information reaching us people continue to be killed daily by shelling and aerial bombing, which includes the use of cluster bombs. We hope that international organisations, such as United Nations, will intervene to stop this carnage. When people are in danger, everyone has a duty to speak out. Unfortunately the people suffering in this current acute crisis are the very same people that have suffered the most from the chronic burden of war discussed in this report. The urgent need to address the immediate and long term rehabilitation of this population must take into consideration enduring health inequalities and will be an enormous challenge.

Mayan Vije and Suppiah Ratneswaren
15 March 2009
London

Executive Summary

Introduction

This evidence-based report by the Tamil Information Centre (TIC) analyses, from a human rights and public health perspective, the impact of the violent conflict in Sri Lanka on health, the health system, and relief and reconstruction. In particular it examines the deteriorating health of the population in the conflict zones of the northern and eastern Provinces.

This report is the fruit of an extensive literature review and discussions with health professionals and health workers in Sri Lanka and elsewhere. It cites and analyses data derived from the reports of international and nongovernmental agencies that have worked in Sri Lanka or been involved with Sri Lanka over many years. TIC has also collected data, and has initiated and facilitated the visits of Sri Lankan expatriate health professionals to assist local agencies and institutions involved in health provision and promotion in war-torn areas of the island.

Data collection in conflict zones is notoriously difficult, and the available information in Sri Lanka is often fragmented, patchy, misleading or biased. The authors have made every effort to construct a robust evidence base in this report, and their conclusions are as authoritative and objective as possible. However, TIC cannot be held responsible for any shortcomings that arise as a result of poor data or inadvertent errors of fact or interpretation. It welcomes corrections and additional information.

Main findings

The effects of war are often measured by death and injuries due to weaponry, and the grim total in Sri Lanka is likely to be at least a quarter of a million deaths and hundreds of thousands of trauma-related injuries. Less attention is usually paid to deaths and illnesses arising from the indirect effects of conflict, but as this report suggests, the longer-term impact on the population of the North-East is likely to be equally dramatic. Health has been harmed by conflict-related damage to health-sustaining infrastructure and the health system, as well as by the corrosive effects of conflict-related factors such as poverty, unemployment, disrupted education and low morale.

Our examination of the health of the population in the North-East of Sri Lanka suggests that a wide range of factors have had a major and negative impact on health. These include:

25 years of violent conflict;
an economic embargo;
continuous population displacement;
human rights violations by all parties in the conflict;
inadequate health facilities;
shortages of staff, medicines and medical equipment;
harassment of humanitarian workers and agencies;
use of humanitarian aid as a weapon of war;
deliberate discrimination on ethnic grounds.

The Sri Lankan constitution guarantees freedom of movement but this right has been severely curtailed for the country's Tamil population, particularly in the North-East. Since 1990, restrictions on food, medicines, fuel, materials for education, commerce, agriculture and industry have seriously affected the economy in the North-East of the country. Checkpoints, restricted zones, military camps and prohibited areas have affected all aspects of life and eroded rights, including the right to health. Agents of the state, including the police and the army, have attacked human rights defenders (including health workers) through murder, disappearances, assaults, injury, torture and death threats.

The Sri Lankan state and a succession of governments have violated human rights and undermined the rule of law. People cannot exercise their legitimate rights and carry on their daily lives with freedom and dignity. Security forces and groups aligned to the government have been involved in extra-judicial killings, illegal detention, torture, disappearances and rape. Some medical personnel are implicated in torture and others turn a blind eye to torture and degrading treatment. Successive governments have failed to take adequate measures to curb violations, compensate victims of abuse or punish the perpetrators, and have thus encouraged impunity. They have also introduced or maintained draconian legislation such as the Prevention of Terrorism Act (PTA) and Emergency Regulations (ER), in force for more than 30 years despite international concern, and used almost exclusively against the Tamil community.

Military operations have caused large-scale displacement of the Tamil population in the North-East. Following pressure from the Sri Lankan government many humanitarian agencies have been forced to leave the region amd sometimes the country. Access to internally displaced persons (IDPs) and freedom of movement for civilians, humanitarian agency staff and relief supplies are among the most prominent challenges confronting aid agencies.

The conflict and associated trauma have created huge psychological problems, which are more common in displaced families. Repeated displacement and disruption of livelihoods have made people dependent on handouts. Women often have to take on extra responsibilities without adequate support, making them particularly vulnerable.

Shortages of food and medicine have badly affected vulnerable people in the North-East, including the elderly, the disabled, widows, people traumatized by war and the tsunami, children and IDPs. In 2007, some districts were classified by the World Food Programme as being in 'acute food and livelihood crisis' owing to armed conflict and the government embargo on fuel, agricultural and construction materials. Jaffna and Batticaloa districts, classified as a 'humanitarian emergency', faced a widespread high-intensity conflict with thousands of IDPs, collapsing markets and increasing malnutrition.

Public health infrastructure and health care facilities, goods and services are not available in sufficient quantity or quality, leading to a severe shortage of safe drinking water and adequate sanitation, trained health staff and essential drugs. The quality of health services is far below the rest of the island. Medicines received from Colombo are often out of date. There are nursing schools in Jaffna and Batticaloa, but Tamils are discriminated against in the selection process conducted by the Ministry of Health. In 2002 the World Health Organisation (WHO) confirmed that shortages of health personnel, basic facilities and support systems had impeded health care delivery in the North-East.

Security forces were directly responsible for destroying many institutions, while others have been closed for lack of staff and drugs or for security reasons. By 2002, 56 out of 405 health institutions in the North-East had been destroyed and 51 were not functioning. Hospitals and health centres are dilapidated and deteriorating. Most buildings are 50-80 years old with inadequate water supplies and sewage systems, and a lack of equipment and supplies. Preventive health measures have also been severely affected by a lack of basic facilities and support.

The international community has responded with humanitarian assistance for North-East Sri Lanka, despite the lack of a safe humanitarian space in which they can operate. $4.5 billion in aid for reconstruction was pledged by the 51 nations and 22 international agencies that participated in the 2003 Tokyo Conference on Reconstruction and Development of Sri Lanka. The conference co-chairs - Japan, the US, the European Union and Norway - were appointed to monitor and review progress in the peace process. However this process has regularly been disrupted by renewed outbreaks of fighting, with both parties to the conflict accused of ignoring ceasefire agreements.

Sri Lanka's national health statistics show consistent improvements in health. However the demographic and health information on which they are based often excludes the conflict zones. The data scrutinized in this report, including detailed situation analyses from a variety of sources, reflect the impact of the conflict. There are wide inequalities between people in the North-East and elsewhere in Sri Lanka, and between IDPs and the rest of the population. The infant mortality rate in the North-East is much higher than the island-wide average. Maternal deaths have been falling in the rest of the country, but increasing in the North-East. Nutritional surveys of children under 5 show a similar pattern. The lack of basic facilities and support which has impeded the delivery of preventive care, has contributed to inequalities in the rates of malaria and other diseases.

Conclusion

This report highlights the failure of all sides in the conflict to protect health, or to facilitate the rebuilding of the health system. It describes the devastating direct and indirect impacts of the conflict particularly for those living in the North-East but also for Sri Lanka as a whole. Conflict, criminality, social inequality, lack of democratic processes, political instability and decrepit essential infrastructure combine to damage health and arrest the development of a decentralised, primary care-based health system. Immediate action is needed: the need to find alternatives to violence and to resolve political differences peacefully, not least so that ordinary people can rebuild their shattered lives, could not be more urgent.

Recommendations

The Tamil Information Centre, deeply concerned by the conclusions of this report, makes the following recommendations:

(1) We call upon the Government of Sri Lanka, the LTTE leadership and the international community to take urgent measures to address the humanitarian crisis in northern Sri Lanka; to ensure that the whole population receives adequate food, fuel, medical supplies and supplies for agriculture, industry and fisheries; and to provide IDPs with shelter and security.

Recommendations to the Government of Sri Lanka

(2) We urge the Government of Sri Lanka to bring the economic blockade of the North-East region to an immediate end and allow the supply of all materials needed for education, health, sanitation and economic activity.

(3) We urge the Government of Sri Lanka to end the pursuit of a military solution, and to take measures to resolve the political deadlock, including discussions on substantial devolution of power to the North-East region on the basis of the Oslo Declaration of 2002.

(4) We urge the Government of Sri Lanka to end all discrimination based on race, ethnicity or other grounds and ensure that all people, including the population of the North-East, enjoy the right to life, health and other human rights, including:
access to adequate food, clean water, housing, employment, education, and health facilities; the right to human dignity, equality, privacy, freedom of information, association, assembly and movement; the right to benefit from scientific progress and its applications.

(5) We urge the Government of Sri Lanka to remove restrictions on the freedom of movement, to enable people to engage freely in social and economic activities, and to gain access to health facilities.

(6) We urge the Government of Sri Lanka to make available to the population of the North-East adequate and functioning public health services and healthcare facilities, goods and services; and to provide adequate funds to rebuild, repair or refurbish existing facilities.

Recommendations to the international community

Considering that the right to health is dependent on, and contributes to, the realization of many other human rights:

(7) We call on the UN and the international community to continue to press for access by an international human rights monitoring body to all parts of Sri Lanka and relevant institutions, with a view to improving human rights and ensuring all actors in Sri Lanka observe their human rights obligations and commitments.

(8) We call on the UN and the international community to ensure that a mechanism for the investigation of human rights violations throughout the island is established, with international participation, which meets the requirements of independence, credibility, effectiveness and empowerment, and thus contributes to public confidence, peace and stability in all parts of Sri Lanka.

(9) We call on the UN and the international community to ensure that impunity (exemption from punishment or loss) for state officials and members of the security forces is ended in Sri Lanka, paying special attention to the laws and regulations that contribute to impunity, particularly through proper, impartial investigations of alleged torture, rape, disappearances and extra-judicial executions; and that all perpetrators, irrespective of ethnic origin, position or status, are prosecuted.

(10) We call on the UN and the international community to urge the Sri Lankan government to recognize the role of human rights defenders in the protection of human rights and fundamental freedoms; to end all verbal and physical attacks on human rights defenders; and to promote a mechanism for the protection of human rights defenders so they can carry out their work unimpeded.

(11) We call on the UN, the Co-Chairs of the Tokyo Conference*, governments and all other relevant bodies to exert greater pressure on the Sri Lankan government and the Liberation Tigers of Tamil Eelam (LTTE) to return to the negotiating table and continue negotiations until a political settlement is reached.

Recommendations to UN organizations working on health

Considering that discrimination in access to health services based on race has continued in Sri Lanka for several decades:

(12) We request the World Health Organization (WHO), other relevant UN bodies and international agencies to review their policies and programmes in relation to Sri Lanka, to ensure that all people are treated equally and have equal access to health facilities.

(13) We request the UN Special Rapporteur on the right to the highest attainable standard of physical and mental health, and the Special Rapporteur on the right to food, to investigate discrimination in these areas in Sri Lanka, and the UN Human Rights Council to take appropriate measures based on their findings.

(14) We request WHO, other relevant UN bodies and international agencies to facilitate the study of the impact of war on health in Sri Lanka, so that research can be carried out in the affected regions as a basis for planning and the provision of greater assistance to these regions.

(15) We request WHO, other relevant UN bodies and international agencies to urge the Sri Lankan government to enable the training of more specialists in forensic medicine and in human rights promotion, and to ensure protection for doctors and specialists in these areas.

1 Introduction

1.1 About this report
Scope and aims of this report: sources of information and considerations

This report examines the health conditions in Sri Lanka and the impact of war and war-related security measures on the health of the civilian population. The health of the North-East population has been dispropoortionately affected and there is limited literature on the global health needs of this population. Therefore this report focuses on discrimination in health provision, the state of health infrastructure and the response to essential health needs in North-East Sri Lanka. It describes the human rights situation in North-East Sri Lanka and the failure of the authorities to take adequate measures to protect human rights. It details the situation of internally displaced people (IDPs) and the concern expressed by international agencies on the humanitarian situation. It concludes with recommendations to the Sri Lankan government and the international community.

This report aims to inform a wide audience about the health situation in North-East Sri Lanka, and seeks to improve the health conditions through greater awareness and subsequent action. It is the fruit of a literature review and discussions with health professionals and health workers in Sri Lanka and elsewhere. It cites and analyses data derived from the reports of local and international nongovernmental agencies that have worked in Sri Lanka or have been involved with Sri Lanka over many years. The Tamil Information Centre (TIC) has in this regard initiated and facilitated the visits of Sri Lankan expatriate health professionals to assist local agencies and institutions involved in health provision and promotion in war-torn areas of the island.

Data collection in conflict zones is notoriously difficult and – as discussed below - the available information in Sri Lanka is often fragmented, patchy, misleading or biased. The authors have made every effort to construct a robust evidence base in this report, and their conclusions are as authoritative and objective as possible. However the TIC cannot be held responsible for any shortcomings that arise as a result of poor data, inadvertent errors of fact or interpretation, and welcomes all corrections and additions.

1.2 About Sri Lanka
Background history and demographic profile

Sri Lanka (formerly Ceylon), an island nation in the Indian Ocean, lies 25 miles (40 kilometres) southeast of southern India. It is 25,000 square miles (65,000 square kilometres) in extent and has an estimated population of 19 million (see Table 1). Of the major ethnic groups, Sinhalese constitute approximately 74% of the population, Tamils around 18% and Muslims 7%. (The term 'Muslim' is used in Sri Lanka to describe people of Arab descent, so signifies an ethnic as well as religious identity; the term is used in the same sense in this report). Two distinct groupings are recognized among the Tamils. The Sri Lankan Tamils comprise about 12% of the population and mainly live in the North-East. The Plantation Tamils, whose predecessors were brought by the British from southern India to work on the coffee, tea and rubber plantations, comprise around 6% and mainly live in the hill country of the central provinces. The language of the Sinhalese is Sinhala; Tamils and most Muslims speak Tamil. Four major religions are practised – approximately 70% of the population is Buddhist, 15% Hindu, 7% Muslim and 7% Christian. A large number of Tamils are Hindu and most Sinhalese are Buddhist.

The historical origins of the communities are hotly debated but according to modern historians the Sinhalese and Sri Lankan Tamil groups are descendants of the Mesolithic people who occupied almost all the island in prehistoric times (Indrapala 2005). The origins of the Muslim community can be traced back to Arab traders who frequented the island's ports even before the birth of Islam (Ali 1997). The political history of Sri Lanka in the centuries before the arrival of the European powers is largely a chronicle of the rise and fall of individual kingdoms. When the first westerners, the Portuguese, arrived in 1505, there were four kingdoms: the Kotte and Sitawaka kingdoms in the south, the Jaffna kingdom in the north and the Kandyan kingdom in the central hills. The Portuguese invaded the Jaffna kingdom in 1619 and went on to control the coastal provinces, but the Kandyan kingdom remained independent. The Dutch captured Colombo from the Portuguese in 1656, and by 1766 had full control of the coastal provinces. The Dutch-held territory was surrendered to the British in 1796, and Sri Lanka was confirmed as a British colony by the 1802 Peace of Amiens. British forces seized the Kandyan kingdom in 1815. Sri Lanka gained independence from the United Kingdom in 1948.

Table 1 Facts about Sri Lanka

Area (sq km)	65,610
Population 2006	19,886,000[1]
Male population 2006	9,826,000[1]
Female population 2006	10,060,000[1]
Population density 2006	317[1]
Population growth rate 2006	1.1[1]
GNI per capita 2006 (US$)	3,730[2]
Life expectancy – **male** (years)	68.8[2]
Life expectancy – female (years)	76.3[2]
Adult literacy rate 2000-2005	91[3]

Map 1 Sri Lanka & India

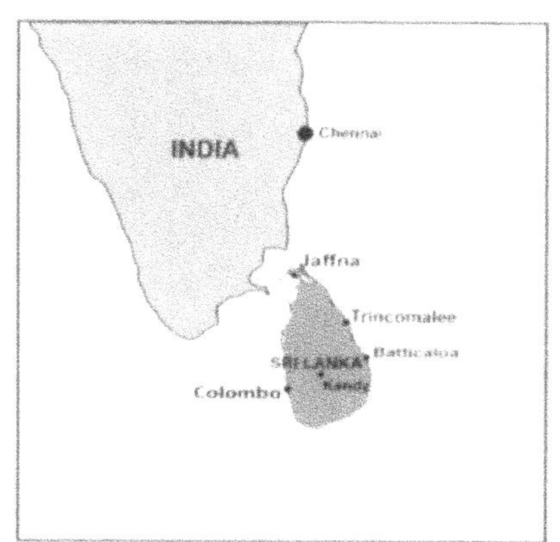

Sources:
1. Department of Census and Statistics, Sri Lanka (www.statistics.gov.org)
2. UNFPA 2008
3. UNICEF

Map 2 Sri Lanka and the North & East Provinces

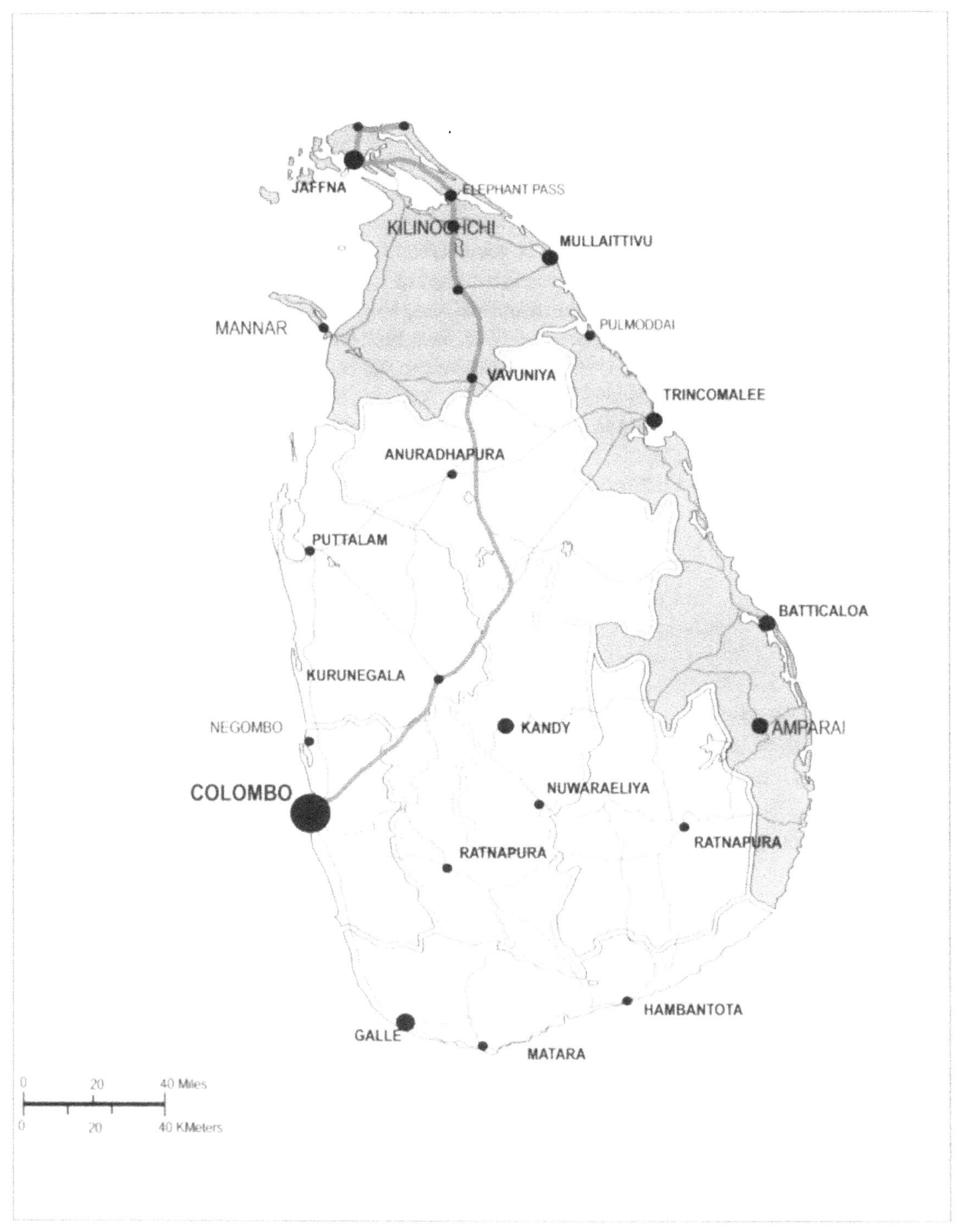

1.3 A history of violent conflict

Origins of the conflict; a history of failed negotiations; the Oslo Declaration ignored; a desperate human rights situation

The current political tensions between the Sinhalese and Tamil can be traced back to 1883 when the British administration brought three ancient kingdoms under one unitary state. Since independence, the growth of Sinhalese nationalism culminated in discriminatory language, education and employment policies, state-aided Sinhala settlements in Tamil areas, and anti-Tamil pogroms. In response, Tamil parliamentarians advocated for equal rights and autonomy in the largely Tamil-speaking regions of the North-East. However, successive Sinhalese governments (led by the United National Party and Sri Lanka Freedom Party) repeatedly backed out of promises, which resulted in growing radicalization among Tamils (Levy and Sidel 2008). The growing support for the Liberation Tigers of Tamil Eelam (LTTE) had led to the longest on-going civil wars.

Violent conflict since 1983 has had a disastrous effect on development and has led to extreme hardship and suffering. The North-East of the country has been devastated not only by the war but also by the 2004 tsunami. Sri Lanka is a country of rich cultural, ethnic and religious diversity and the causes of conflict are many: they include discrimination against minorities by successive parliaments and governments in education, employment, use of language and economic development; failure to adopt national policies promoting unity, equality, mutual understanding and trust; failure by governments to honour agreements reached with Tamil leaders; and periodic and large-scale violence against Tamils since 1956. Thousands of civilians, the vast majority Tamils, have died and hundreds of families have been forced to seek refuge in other part of the country or abroad. Successive governments have implemented programmes of state-aided colonization of the Tamil areas. These have occurred simultaneously with campaigns of violence with attempt to change demographic patterns and destroy Tamil identity.

Box 1 highlights the succession of failed ceasefires and peace talks. Peace negotiations in 1985, 1989 and 1994 ended in failure, but the 2002 ceasefire agreement between the government and the Liberation Tigers of Tamil Eelam (LTTE), agreed with significant input from the international community, kindled hopes of an end to the conflict. Norway was nominated as facilitator of the ceasefire monitoring process, and an international monitoring team of representatives from Nordic countries - the Sri Lanka Monitoring Mission (SLMM) - was appointed. Following the 2002 Oslo Declaration (see Box 2) the international community pledged aid for rehabilitation and reconstruction of the North-East. The 2003 Tokyo Conference on the Reconstruction and Development of Sri Lanka brought together 51 nations and 22 international agencies, who pledged $4.5 billion for reconstruction. The decisions of the conference are contained in the Tokyo Declaration. In view of the links between donor support and the peace process, the conference Co-Chairs - Japan, the US, the European Union and Norway - were appointed to monitor and review progress in the peace process.

The optimism was short-lived: no substantial agreement for a lasting solution was reached, and the final round of negotiations in 2006 ended in acrimony. The ceasefire agreement was violated throughout the ceasefire period, and fighting broke out again later that year. The present government has made clear its intention to pursue a military solution. Following verbal attacks on the Norwegian peace facilitators it withdrew from the ceasefire agreement on 16 January 2008, forcing the SLMM to leave the country.

Box 1 Repeated failures to make peace, 1985-2008

- Ceasefire brokered by India began, 18 June 1985
- Peace talks commenced in Bhutan, 8 July 1985
- Agreement signed between India and Sri Lanka, 29 July 1987
- Cessation of hostilities began, 31 July 1987
- Fighting broke out between LTTE and Indian Peace-Keeping Force, 9 October 1987
- Ceasefire between Sri Lankan government and LTTE began, 27 June 1989
- Withdrawal of the Indian Peace Keeping Force from Sri Lanka, 31 March 1990
- Fighting broke out between LTTE and government forces, 11 June 1990
- Cessation of hostilities announced between LTTE and government, 6 January 1995
- Fighting broke out between LTTE and government forces, 19 April 1995
- LTTE ceasefire announcement, 19 December 2001
- Sri Lankan government ceasefire reciprocation, 24 December 2001
- Ceasefire agreement (brokered by Norway) between LTTE and government, 22 February 2002
- Fighting broke out between LTTE and government forces, 26 July 2006
- Sri Lankan government withdrew from ceasefire agreement, 16 January 2008

The government has ignored the principles of the Oslo Declaration and has refused to allow international monitoring of human rights. The UN and other agencies have documented the involvement of state officials and government security forces in assassinations, abductions, disappearances, torture, illegal arrests and detentions, and child recruitment. The government has encouraged impunity among the security forces and has been responsible for the deaths of hundreds of Tamil and other civilians, including children, indiscriminate shelling and aerial bombardment. For its part the LTTE has carried out extra-judicial executions, indiscriminate attacks on civilians, assassinations, disappearances and child recruitment.

Sri Lanka is accused of being the third most dangerous place in the world for journalists (Press Emblem Campaign 2007), while the UN says it is a very dangerous place for aid workers (Reuters 2007). The provisions of the US law suspending arms supply to Sri Lanka, which came into effect in 2008, requested the government to bring to justice members of the military who have committed gross violations of human rights or international humanitarian law, including complicity in the recruitment of child soldiers; to provide access to humanitarian organizations and journalists throughout the country consistent with international humanitarian law; and to agree to the establishment of a local field presence of the Office of the United Nations High Commissioner for Human Rights (OHCHR), with sufficient staff and mandate to conduct full and unfettered monitoring throughout the country and to publicize its findings (US Congress 2007).

Box 2 The Oslo Declaration, 2002

The 2002 Oslo Declaration was accepted as a basis for a political solution to the conflict by both parties of the conflict and the international community. The parties agreed to explore a solution founded on the principle of internal self-determination in areas of historical habitation of the Tamil-speaking peoples, based on a federal structure within a united Sri Lanka. The term 'areas of historical habitation' refers to the Northern and Eastern Provinces, claimed by Tamils as the Tamil homeland. The term 'Tamil-speaking people' includes Tamils and Muslims.

The President of Sri Lanka appointed an All Party Representative Committee (APRC) in June 2006 with a mandate to prepare devolution proposals that would be the basis for a solution to the conflict. The APRC has consistently opposed institutional devolution of power to Tamil areas, and has undermined discussions by promoting a minority report from the Sri Lankan Expert Committee on Devolution.

In May 2008 the UN General Assembly turned down Sri Lanka's application for re-election to serve on the UN Human Rights Council (UNHRC), an acknowledgement of both Sri Lanka's failure to discharge its international obligations in relation to human rights and the lack of independence, transparency and accountability in national human rights mechanisms. Despite international condemnation, the government has continued to deny human rights in the North-East and has occasionally launched attacks on the UN. It is virtually impossible for journalists to gain access to conflict zones (Reporters sans Frontières 2008). An international mission in 2006 found that the Tamil-language media have borne the brunt of the government-led assault on the press, particularly in the North-East (International Freedom of Expression Exchange 2006).

2 The right to life and health

2.1 State obligations

The right to the highest attainable standard of health and the Geneva Conventions; the consequences of disregarding them

According to the preamble of the constitution of the World Health Organization (WHO), the enjoyment of the highest attainable standard of health is "one of the fundamental rights of every human being without distinction of race, religion, political belief, economic or social condition". It also states that "the health of all peoples is fundamental to the attainment of peace and security and is dependent upon the fullest co-operation of individuals and States". The obligation to respect the right to health requires states to refrain from denying or limiting equal access to health services, and from enforcing discriminatory practices as state policy.

The Geneva Conventions and their Additional Protocols stipulate the respect and protection of people wounded, sick and shipwrecked, regardless of whether they have taken part in the conflict. They should be treated humanely in all circumstances and receive the medical care and attention required by their condition, to the fullest extent practicable and with the least possible delay; there should be no distinction between persons other than on medical grounds. The Conventions prohibit starvation of civilians as a method of combat, and attacking, destroying, removing or rendering useless, for that purpose, objects indispensable to the survival of civilians, such as foodstuffs, agricultural areas for the production of foodstuffs, crops, livestock, drinking water installations and supplies, and irrigation works. When international humanitarian law and the right to health are not upheld, children are often the most vulnerable, and Box 3 describes the failure to protect children's rights in the North-East.

Box 3 Threats to children's rights and well-being

"Severe acute malnutrition (SAM) among under-five children in parts of conflict-affected Batticaloa and Jaffna districts is 6 per cent and 6.7 per cent respectively (2007), while the country prevalence is 2.5 per cent (Demographic and Health Survey 2000). Access to potable water and to safe sanitation stands at 79 per cent and 76 per cent respectively, for the entire population. However, in some conflict-affected districts, sanitation coverage is as low as 30 per cent (2007).

More than a quarter of a million primary school-aged children are partially and/or completely out of the education system. The resumption of open fighting has increased the risk of underage recruitment by armed groups and other child rights' violations related to conflict. Displacement and pervasive indiscriminate violence, including claymore attacks, landmines/unexploded ordnance and aerial bombings have resulted in a climate of fear and significant disparity in vulnerable areas."

Source: UNICEF 2008

2.2 Determinants of health
The underlying determinants of health and their link to the right to health

The right to health refers to a wide range of factors that promote a healthy life. These underlying determinants of health include safe drinking water and adequate sanitation; safe food; adequate nutrition and housing; healthy working and environmental conditions; health-related education and information; and gender equality (UN Committee on Economic, Social and Cultural Rights 2000).

These determinants protect and promote the right to health far beyond health services and thus the right to health depends on and contributes to the realization of many other human rights. These include the rights to food, water, an adequate standard of living, adequate housing, freedom from discrimination, privacy, access to information, participation, the freedoms of association, assembly and movement, and the right to benefit from scientific progress and its applications (WHO and Office of the UN High Commissioner for Human Rights 2008). Four essential elements comprise the right to health care: availability, accessibility, acceptability and quality, as described in Box 4.

2.3 Violations of human rights and the rule of law
State obligations in relation to human rights: a history of violation

Human rights are interdependent, indivisible and interrelated, so violating the right to health often impairs the realisation of other human rights and vice versa (WHO and Office of the UN High Commissioner for Human Rights 2008). States bear ultimate responsibility as guarantors of democracy, human rights and the rule of law, and are obliged to promote respect for and observance of human rights and freedoms (UN Committee on Economic, Social and Cultural Rights 2000). Sri Lanka has ratified several international human rights instruments and thereby agreed to be accountable to its citizens and the international community for fulfilling its obligations under these instruments. By signing the International Covenant on Economic, Social and Cultural Rights, Sri Lanka recognizes the universal right to the enjoyment of the highest attainable standard of physical and mental health and to an adequate standard of living, including adequate food, clothing and housing, and to the continuous improvement of living conditions. By ratifying the International Convention on the Elimination of All Forms of Racial Discrimination, Sri Lanka agrees to guarantee the enjoyment of economic, social and cultural rights without discrimination, including the rights to public health, medical care, social security and social services, housing, education and training, and equal participation in cultural activities.

States are also obliged to guarantee human rights and fundamental freedoms without discrimination, and to subject rights only to such limitations solely for the purpose of promoting the general welfare in a democratic society. States must uphold their human rights obligations during periods of conflict and national emergency, in accordance with international law, the rule of law, and the principles of democracy (UN Human Rights Commission 2005).

Box 4 Essential elements of the right to health

(a) Availability. Functioning public health and healthcare facilities, goods and services, as well as programmes, have to be available in sufficient quantity. They include the underlying determinants of health, such as safe and potable drinking water and adequate sanitation facilities, hospitals, clinics and other health-related buildings, trained personnel receiving domestically competitive salaries, and essential drugs.

(b) Accessibility. Health facilities, goods and services have to be accessible to everyone without discrimination, within the jurisdiction of the state party. Accessibility has four overlapping dimensions:

Non-discrimination: health facilities, goods and services must be accessible to all, especially the most vulnerable or marginalized sections of the population...and in fact, without discrimination on any of the prohibited grounds.

Physical accessibility: health facilities, goods and services must be within safe physical reach for all sections of the population, especially vulnerable or marginalized groups, such as ethnic minorities and indigenous populations, women, children, adolescents, older persons, people with disabilities and people with HIV/AIDS.

Economic accessibility (affordability): health facilities, goods and services must be affordable by all. Payment for healthcare services, as well as services related to the wider determinants of health, has to be based on the principle of equity, ensuring that these services, whether privately or publicly provided, are affordable by all, including socially disadvantaged groups.

Information accessibility: accessibility includes the right to seek, receive and impart information and ideas concerning health issues. However, accessibility of information should not impair the right to have personal health data treated with confidentiality.

(c) Acceptability: All health facilities, goods and services must be respectful of medical ethics and culturally appropriate, i.e. respectful of the culture of individuals, minorities, peoples and communities; sensitive to gender and life-cycle requirements; and designed to respect confidentiality and improve the health status of those concerned.

(d) Quality: As well as being culturally acceptable, health facilities, goods and services must also be scientifically and medically appropriate and of good quality. This requires, inter alia, skilled personnel, scientifically approved and unexpired drugs and hospital equipment, safe and potable water, and adequate sanitation.

Source: UN Committee on Economic, Social and Cultural Rights 2000

Sri Lankan governments have violated human rights and undermined the rule of law (UN Human Rights Council 2006), and people are unable to exercise their legitimate rights and carry on their lives without fear, in freedom and dignity. Successive governments have failed to take adequate measures to curb violations, compensate victims of abuses or punish the perpetrators, and have thus encouraged impunity among the security forces and state officers. The governments have also introduced and maintained draconian legislation, used almost exclusively against the Tamil community, for more than 30 years since independence. The abuse of human rights has been widely condemned by the international community, as shown in the examples below dating from 1983 to the present.

Documented human rights abuse, 1983-2008

1983 "Amnesty International (AI) knows of no criminal prosecutions of officials believed to have been responsible for extra-judicial killings in Sri Lanka since July 1983, not even in respect of the 51 such killings in late July 1983, for which the government itself has acknowledged responsibility" (AI 1984).

1985 "Amnesty International are concerned about reports of random killings of non-combatant Tamil civilians by members of the security forces. It also remained concerned about the detention of Tamils, members of left-wing opposition parties and students under legislation permitting long-term detention without charge or trial. It continued to receive reports of widespread torture of detainees. Several reports of deaths in custody, allegedly as a result of torture or shooting were received" (AI 1985).

1987 "Amnesty International is gravely concerned.....that at least 150 civilians, nearly all Tamils, have been deliberately killed by members of the Special Task Force in Batticaloa during a military operation starting 28 January 1987. That day, 13 STF men were killed, most in a landmine attributed to armed Tamil separatists" (AI 1987).

1990 The UN Special Rapporteur on Extrajudicial, Summary and Arbitrary Executions (1991) report the disappearance of 158 Tamils taken into custody by Sri Lankan security forces from the Vantharumoolai refugee camp.

1991 Amnesty International report that "scores of people were extra-judicially executed and several hundred 'disappeared', probable victims of torture and shooting in custody... The military, the police and the Special Task Force police commando unit were responsible for scores of extrajudicial executions in the North-East... Some victims were people who have spoken out against violations committed by the security forces" (AI 1992).

1993 Amnesty International note that scores of civilians were reportedly killed during the year by the security forces, some apparently victims of extrajudicial executions, as they attempted to cross the Kilali lagoon. "In some cases, navy personnel reportedly boarded boats and deliberately killed civilian passengers who offered no resistance... Civilians were also reportedly targeted in reprisal bombing raids in Jaffna. Ten civilians reportedly died and about 30 were injured on 13 November when two air force jets bombed St James' church in the centre of Jaffna town" (AI 1994).

1995 Amnesty International express concern about continuing reports of arbitrary arrests, torture, rape, disappearances and extrajudicial executions (AI 1995).

1998 The UN Special Rapporteur on Extrajudicial, Summary or Arbitrary Executions (1998) report periodical extrajudicial executions, but few perpetrators brought to justice. "This culture of impunity has led to arbitrary killings and has contributed to the uncontrollable spiralling of violence. The systematic absence of investigation, either civil or military, into violations of the right to life facilitates impunity. Investigations are rarely conducted, and when they are, they do not lead to the appropriate convictions or penalties... Several relatives of disappeared people and human rights organizations from all areas of Sri Lanka have expressed concern that many members of the security forces and others allegedly responsible for grave human rights violations in the recent past continue to hold official posts in the same areas where the violations took place and may try to interfere with the investigations".

1998 The UN Committee against Torture (1998) are "gravely concerned by the serious violations of the Convention against Torture in Sri Lanka, particularly regarding torture linked with disappearances".

2000 The UN Special Rapporteur on Violence against Women express concern that the incidence of gang rape and murder of women and girls by Sri Lankan soldiers continue unabated (UN press release 2000).

2000 The UN Working Group on Enforced or Involuntary Disappearances (2000) said Sri Lanka remained the country with the second largest number of unclarified disappearances in the world. It had received reports of 12,277 disappearances between 1980 and 2000, of which 11,682 remained unclarified.

2003 The UN Human Rights Committee (2003) "remain concerned about persistent reports of torture, and cruel, inhuman or degrading treatment or punishment of detainees by law enforcement officials and members of the armed forces, and about the intimidation or threat of victims, thereby discouraging them from pursuing effective remedy".

2005 The UN Committee against Torture (2005) express concern about non-observance of fundamental legal safeguards such as habeas corpus; continued well-documented allegations of widespread torture, ill-treatment and disappearances, mainly committed by the Sri Lankan police forces; the lack of effective, systematic review of places of detention; continued allegations of sexual violence and abuse of women and children in custody, including by law enforcement officials; undue delay of trials, especially trials of people accused of torture and reprisals; intimidation and threats against persons reporting acts of torture and ill-treatment; and lack of effective witness and victim protection mechanisms.

2000 The Asian Human Rights Commission say many Tamil and Muslim civilians have been killed, "primarily because they have sought to exercise their freedoms of expression, movement, association, and participation in ways that are not supportive of one or other of the factions fighting the Government… Almost none of these extrajudicial executions have been effectively investigated. Police and military investigations into the killing of Tamils or the broader range of deaths in custody have too often been poorly handled and remarkably few convictions have resulted… The failure to effectively prosecute government violence is a deeply-felt problem in Sri Lanka. The paucity of cases in which a government official - such as a soldier or police officer - has been convicted for the killing of a Tamil is an example" (AHRC 2000, 2006).

2007 Following a visit to Sri Lanka, the UN Special Rapporteur on Torture and other cruel, inhuman or degrading treatment or punishment notes indications that torture was widely practised – "the high number of indictments for torture filed by the Attorney General's office, the number of successful fundamental rights cases decided by the Supreme Court, as well as the high number of complaints that the National Human Rights Commission continues to receive almost daily" (UN press release 2007).

2008 Under intense criticism for its human rights record, Sri Lanka's application for re-election to the UN Human Rights Council is turned down by the UN General Assembly on 21 May 2008. This was a clear indication that the world was beginning to learn of the enormous repression and to condemn it: "that the country with the largest number of disappearances and widespread lawlessness has not been given a place in the leading body on human rights within the UN system is not a surprise" (AHRC 2008).

3 North-East Sri Lanka

Map 3 North-East Sri Lanka - the region of 25 years of civil war

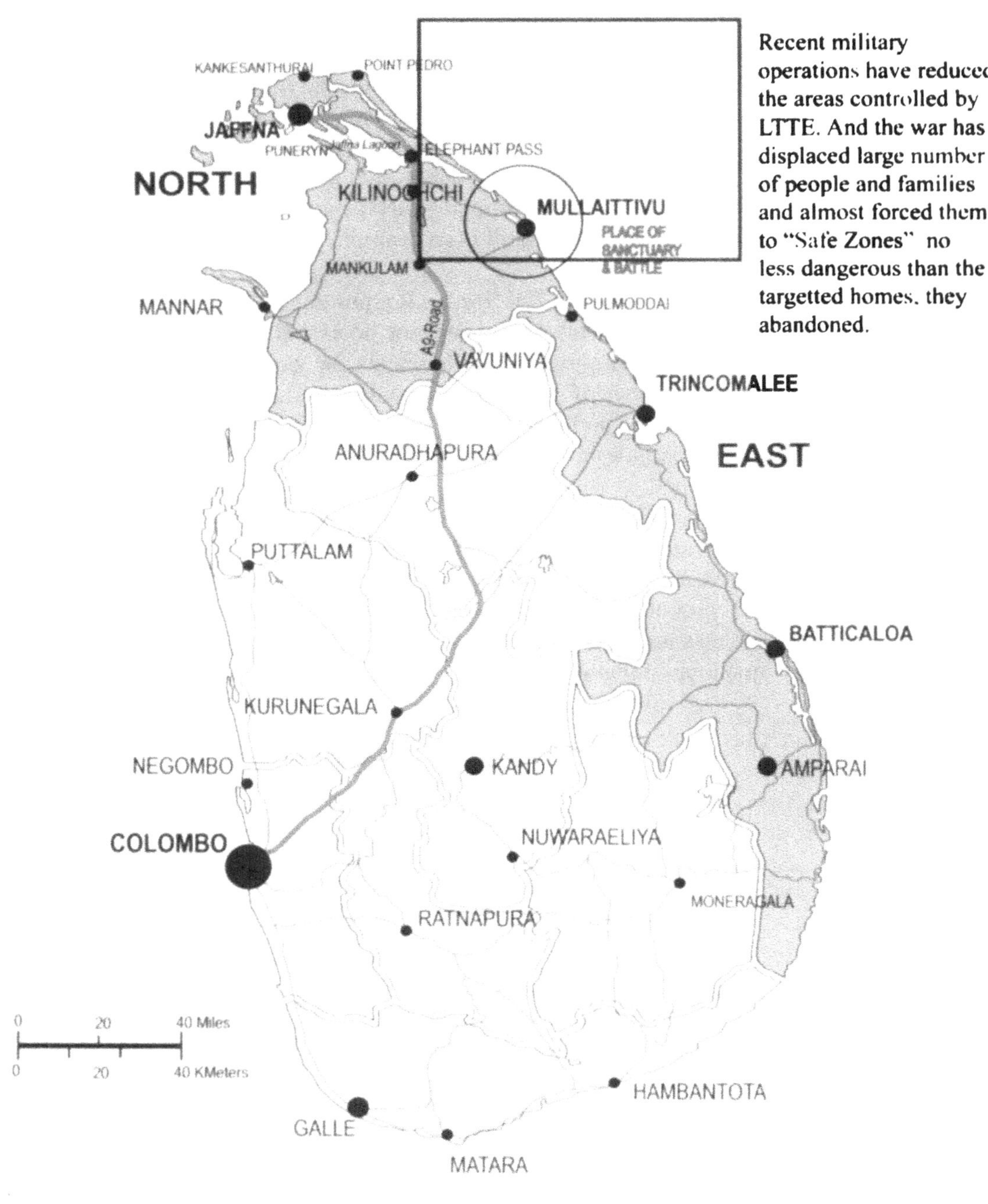

Recent military operations have reduced the areas controlled by LTTE. And the war has displaced large number of people and families and almost forced them to "Safe Zones" no less dangerous than the targetted homes. they abandoned.

3.1 Demography and governance
The geographical and political map of the North-East of Sri Lanka

The northern and eastern regions of Sri Lanka (generally referred to in this report as 'the North-East') comprise the Northern Province, including the districts of Jaffna, Kilinochchi, Mannar, Mullaitivu, and Vavuniya; and the Eastern Province, including the districts of Amparai, Batticaloa and Trincomalee. The Vanni region in the north includes Vavuniya, Mannar and Mullaitivu districts and the part of Kilinochchi district lying on the mainland (the other part of Kilinochchi district lies within the Jaffna peninsula). Table 2 shows regional population data.

Table 2 Area and population, North-East Sri Lanka 2006

	Area	Population	Population %		
	(Sq. Km.)		Tamil	Muslim	Sinhalese
Whole of Sri Lanka	65,610	19,886,000	18	7	73
North-East Sri Lanka	18,640	2,643,000	64*	21*	15*
Eastern Province	9,793	1,540,000	42*	34*	24*
Amparai District	4,431	613,000	19	42	39
Batticaloa District	2,633	544,000	74	24	2
Trincomalee District	2,729	383,000	32	36	32
Northern Province	8,846	1,103,000	94*	3*	3*
Jaffna District	1,023	596,000	99	1†	-
Kilinochchi District	1,237	143,000	100	-	-
Mannar District	2,002	97,000	85	12	3
Mullaitivu District	2,617	125,000	95	-	-
Vavuniya District	1,967	142,000	75	7	18

Note:
* Calculations based on data from North-East Provincial Council and Central Bank of Sri Lanka
† Jaffna's population was 10% Muslim, before they were evicted by the LTTE in 1990. Northern Province district figures are estimates from past trends.
Sources: North-East Provincial Council 2006; Central Bank of Sri Lanka – See Table 1 in Economy of the conflict region in Sri Lanka by Muttukrishna Sarvananthan.

At the time of the ceasefire agreement in February 2002, the LTTE controlled large parts of the North-East, while other areas were under the control of the government. The LTTE operated a parallel administration, establishing a police force, a judicial system and introducing laws, as well as providing some health services. Government offices continued to function in LTTE areas. Government forces captured the LTTE-controlled areas in the Eastern Province in mid-2007 and continue military operations in an attempt to control the Northern Province.

3.2 **The impact of conflict on life and health**

Mortality, morbidity, displacement and the suffering of civilians; embargoes and violations of the Geneva Conventions; escalating health needs including from the tsunami; an obstructed post-tsunami response; abuse of emergency rule and the predominance of the Ministry of Defence; 2002 assessment shows severe and acute needs

The number of conflict-related deaths between 1985 and 2002 are estimated to be 220,000 (Obermeyer et al 2008) and the vast majority of these are Tamils. In February 2009, Human Rights Watch reported 7000 casualties and 2,000 deaths since the escalation of war just one month earlier (2009), and the daily increase in these numbers continues. The impact on children in particular is described in Box 5.

Nearly 194,000 people have been displaced, mostly Tamil and Muslim civilians (UNHCR 2008a). The economy of the North-East has been seriously affected by embargoes imposed between 1990 and 2001, and the government imposed new restrictions on materials and aid workers in September 2008. UN Secretary-General Ban Ki-Moon, expressing concern over the escalating violence and its humanitarian impact, has called for the safety and freedom of movement of civilians as well as humanitarian organizations, so they are able to work safely and reach those who need humanitarian assistance (UN press release 2008).

The international medical aid agency Médecins sans Frontières has also expressed concern: "civilians caught in the middle of fighting in Sri Lanka's North-East regions live in terror and their day-to-day life is made increasingly precarious by targeted bombings, killings, mine attacks, suicide bombings, abductions, forced recruitment, extortion, restrictions on movement and arbitrary arrests," (MSF 2007). MSF note that this dire situation had been compounded by a general attitude of hostility towards humanitarian aid organizations on the part of the government, and that humanitarian aid was increasingly restricted. According to MSF, civilians suffered due to lack of access to life-saving emergency assistance, at a time when areas near the front line had lost nearly all health staff and hospitals cannot treat the wounded (2007).

Twenty-five years of conflict, economic embargoes, restrictions on medicines and medical equipment, harassment of humanitarian workers and agencies, continuous displacement and human rights violations by both sides have had a serious impact on health. The health of people in the North-East continues to deteriorate. WHO has identified the main risks as increases in malaria, acute respiratory infections and diarrhoeal diseases due to inadequate shelter, damaged water and sanitation systems and overcrowding in centres for IDPs, worsening maternal and child health, psychological trauma and disability (WHO 2002). There continues to be a lack of reliable health data.

The 2002 ceasefire brought about a marginal improvement, but both sides' preoccupation with security matters saw continuing restrictions on essential supplies, and ongoing human rights abuses and emasculation of civil society. The 2004 tsunami caused further devastation to the region (see Section 3c below). A Post-Tsunami Operational Management Structure (P-TOMS) for the equitable distribution of aid was agreed between the Sri Lankan government and the LTTE in June 2005, with the support of the international community; however this was effectively destroyed by the Sri Lankan Supreme Court in November 2005.

Government restrictions on food, medicines, fuel, and supplies for education, commerce, agriculture and industry have seriously affected all sectors of the economy in the North-East since 1990. The economic blockade and others forms of discrimination have been able to continue due to the absence of proper political representation for the region, and the government's direct and total control of all political and administrative structures.

The primary decision making body in relation to the region is the Ministry of Defence. Other government agencies such as the Ministry of Health and the Department of Health have no power to make independent decisions even in their areas of expertise; all decisions on implementation of projects by any government institution must have the approval of the Ministry of Defense. In effect there is military rule in the region in both government-controlled and LTTE-held territory. This nonconstitutional arrangement has been underpinned by emergency rule which has been in force in Sri Lanka for 32 of the 60 years since independence – for 11,763 days as of November 2008. In these circumstances, the health situation in the North-East is likely to deteriorate further.

Box 5 Children killed by air force bombing

Children are being displaced, injured and killed by the violence in Sri Lanka. Many schoolgirls lost their lives and dozens were injured when bombs hit a compound in Mullaitivu in August, 2006. UNICEF and the Sri Lankan Monitoring Mission immediately sent staff to the scene. "As our team was driving towards the compound, they encountered many ambulances and vehicles coming away from that direction carrying bodies of children and young people who had been killed and injured," said Joanna van Gerpen, UNICEF Representative in Sri Lanka. "The compound was showing a lot of damage – one building was still burning." The monitoring team reported that 10-12 bombs, possibly more, had been dropped in the area. It visited four hospitals and saw about 100 injured children being treated. Some of them told UNICEF they were in the compound to attend a two-day first-aid training course.

Source: UNICEF 2006c

Armed conflict and government restrictions had inflicted heavy damage on the population and infrastructure of the region by the time of the 2002 ceasefire. The subsequent findings of the World Bank and other international agencies that made an assessment of the impact on health, education and infrastructure are summarized below (Asian Development Bank et al 2003, British Refugee Council 2003).

Health

Out of a total of 400 health institutions 55 were destroyed and 49 were not functioning. The National Immunization Programme was severely constrained by an irregular supply of vaccines and a lack of trained personnel. Hospitals were affected by shortages of essential drugs and the breakdown of the health information and monitoring systems. Malnutrition was common among mothers and children, and anaemia among women, children and adolescent girls. Laboratory and blood bank facilities, blood transfusion services and reproductive healthcare services were inadequate. Conflict and mine-related injuries had increased mental and physical disabilities resulting from trauma, and there were several thousand ex-combatants with disabilities.

The poor state of water and sanitation facilities had exacerbated the situation. In most towns running water was limited to one or two hours per day and in most rural areas water facilities were in a poor state of repair. Pollution and epidemics of typhoid and cholera were reported. Facilities for water distribution, such as bowsers and plastic water-holding tanks, were unavailable. Over 40% of primary schools had no access to water points and of the remaining 60%, many water points did not meet recognized standards of water quality. Approximately two-thirds of schools had no sanitation facilities.

Education

There was a shortage of 4650 Tamil language-medium teachers and 240 Sinhala language-medium teachers; around 40% of the vacancies were for trained primary teachers and English teachers. There were 47% vacancies in Mullaitivu, 40% in Mannar and 31% in Vavuniya, partly because of displacement of teachers due to the war. Around 15,000 classrooms in 500 schools were damaged or destroyed, requiring an estimated 209,000 m2 of additional classroom space and 312,000 m2 of additional space for laboratories, libraries and office rooms. Equipment, IT facilities, laboratories and furniture were needed. The water and sanitation facilities and the electricity supply of many schools needed replacing. There was a lack of facilities for the special needs of children affected by the conflict, literary centres and non-formal education for children whose education had been affected by war.

Housing

Nearly 326,700 houses had been partly or totally damaged. Household assets such as furniture, fixtures and possessions were damaged or destroyed. Nearly 58% of damaged houses were uninhabitable, about half of which were in Jaffna or Batticaloa. It was estimated that 84% (144,890 units) of the houses owned by IDPs were located in the region and nearly 90% of these were damaged during the conflict (43% of the total damaged houses) making it very difficult for IDPs to return. An estimated 12,000-15,000 damaged houses belonged to refugees in camps in India.

Other infrastructure

Only 10-15% of road surfaces were still intact. With the absence of maintenance during conflict, all pavement surfaces had deteriorated and some had entirely disappeared. Road conditions were poor, vehicle-operating speeds were low and vehicle operating costs were high. Road surface damage was exacerbated by the poor road drainage system, and there was a 20-year development gap between the standards of roads in the North-East and the rest of the country. Many bridges needed replacement or repair and 10 new bridges were needed. Three of the four railway lines had suffered serious damage. Sleepers and railway lines were scavenged to form defence works and stations were destroyed. 166 miles of track on the Jaffna and Talaimannar lines needed re-laying, 40 stations and 12 railway bridges needed reconstructing, and signaling and communication systems needed installing. The five commercial ports - Kankesanthurai, Talaimannar and Point Pedro in the north, and Trincomalee and Oluvil in the east - would have to be cleared of wrecks and rehabilitated to support international services and local commercial, industrial, fisheries and agricultural development.

The region needed 100,000 telephone connections in the first 18-24 months after the ceasefire agreement of 2002 and another 600,000 in the following five years. In the north, 90% of the electricity grid had been damaged; 70% of the grid in Vavuniya and Mannar districts suffering damage of 70% and 50% respectively; the systems in Mullaitivu and Kilinochchi were totally destroyed. In the east, a power station under construction at Valaichenai was not completed. Completion and augmentation was needed for continued supply of electricity to Amparai and Batticaloa. About 95 miles of electricity transmission lines between Vavuniya and the north had also been destroyed and links were needed between Valaichenai and Amparai in the east. In addition, 43 buildings and power equipment in the whole of the region had been damaged or destroyed.

Agriculture and fisheries

There had been substantial destruction of standing crops and those around homesteads, as well as farming equipment and infrastructures. A total of 323,700 hectares of land needed irrigation, and over 30% of the 2398 minor irrigation tanks required rehabilitation. There were severe transport problems, particularly in the Vanni and western parts of the east, which increased the cost of agricultural inputs. Restrictions on transport of fuel and fertilizers also affected agriculture. Around 12,000 fishermen's houses, boats, fishing gear and boat engines had been destroyed. Serious damage had also been caused to supporting infrastructures such as harbours, boatyards, net production facilities, ice plants and fuel supply stations.

3.3 The tsunami of 2004

North-East region worst affected; international support for post-tsunami aid agreement (P-TOMS); P-TOMS derailed

The tsunami that devastated the Asian region on 26 December 2004 caused death and destruction on a massive scale in Sri Lanka. The North-East, already scarred by the impact of armed conflict, was particularly badly affected (see Tables 3-5).

Table 3 People affected by the tsunami

Zone	Affected Families	%	Displaced Families	%	Displaced Persons	%
North-East Sri Lanka	109,521	64.2	78,438	75.6	418,265	76.4
South Sri Lanka	61,173	35.8	25,351	24.4	128,929	23.6
Total	170,694	100	103,789	100	547,194	100

Sources: Disaster Management Centre, Sri Lanka; UNHCR 2005

Table 4 Death and destruction caused by the tsunami

Zone	Deaths	%	Missing persons	%	Houses damaged	%
North-East Sri Lanka	20,507	66.8	3,314	67.1	73,817	66.1
South Sri Lanka	10,211	33.2	1,625	32.9	37,864	33.9
Total	30,718	100	4,939	100	111,681	100

Sources: Disaster Management Centre, Sri Lanka; UNHCR 2005

Table 5 Houses damaged and destroyed by the tsunami

	District	Destroyed	Damaged	Total	% of total
Northern Province	Jaffna	6,084	1,114	7,198	6
	Kilinochchi	1,250	4,250	5,500	4
	Mullaitivu	3,400	2,033	5,433	4
Eastern Province	Trincomalee	5,974	10,394	16,368	13
	Batticaloa	15,939	5,079	21,018	16
	Amparai	29,077	6,332	35,409	27
Subtotal		**61,724**	**29,202**	**90,926**	**70**
South Sri Lanka		19,683	19,074	38,757	30
Total		**81,407**	**48,276**	**129,683**	**100**

Sources: Disaster Management Centre, Sri Lanka; UNHCR 2005

The east suffered heavy damage, accounting for 40% of the financial needs. The south needed 30% and the north 20%. The North-East was the worst affected region in relation to coastal communities, ranging from an estimated 35% affected in Kilinochchi to 80% in Mullaitivu and 78% in Amparai, compared with less than 20% of the coastal population affected in southern districts. The tsunami compounded the impact of the civil war on disruption of social structures, high levels of vulnerability, widespread displacement of people of all ethnic groups, and destruction of infrastructure and housing. Around 58% of the total housing stock needed rebuilding or construction (TIC 2005).

Discussions between the government and the LTTE on a joint mechanism for the equitable distribution of tsunami aid culminated in an agreement in June 2005 for the creation of the P-TOMS, but in November the People's Liberation Front (JVP) instituted legal action against the agreement. The Supreme Court issued an interim injunction on key aspects of the agreement and made a number of statements about the importance of P-TOMS, stating that if it was not implemented immediately, urgent humanitarian assistance could not be granted to people in the North-East, "who have suffered and continue to suffer untold hardship and tragedy from the natural disaster". After Mahinda Rajapakse was elected as President in November 2005, the court inexplicably granted an indefinite injunction against the P-TOMS and postponed the enquiry indefinitely (Sri Lanka Supreme Court 2005).

The international community fully supported the creation of P-TOMS and continued to call for it. According to the European Union, an operational and expedient joint mechanism was a critical step towards ensuring that assistance could be delivered urgently and equitably to all affected communities (EU 2005). Bill Clinton, the UN Special Envoy for Tsunami Recovery, reported that failure to reach an accord in Sri Lanka would heighten concerns that people in the North-East had not had equal access to assistance (UN Special Envoy for Tsunami Recovery 2005). Although the region suffered the worst damage, the government was unwilling to take effective measures to alleviate suffering.

Graph 1 Tsunami Damage - Houses by Region

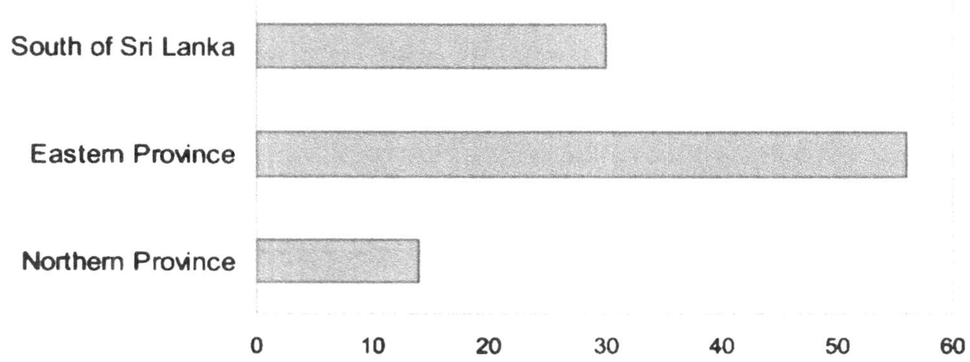

4 Socioeconomic isolation of the North-East

4.1 **Emergency regulations**

Restricted items and the effects on health and livelihoods; prohibited and restricted zones; road closures and curfews; effects on health care, food security and recovery

Successive Sri Lankan governments have used humanitarian aid as a weapon of war. Emergency regulations banning essential items and unofficial restrictions of flow of essential items to the North-East have had serious implications on livlihoods, health resources and access to health. Furthermore, restrictions have extended to humanitarian aid flow. Thus, the populations most affected by the restriction of supplies are also those most isolated from humanitarian aid, because of restrictions on both aid and on freedom of movement.

A blockade on essential materials to the North-East region was introduced by the Ministry of National Security on 1 January 1987. At this point, the Indian delegation to the UN Human Rights Commission expressed concern at Sri Lanka's "unprecedented and extraordinary step of imposing an economic and communications blockade against its own citizens" (UN Human Rights Commission 1987a). Preventing the flow of fuel, firewood and other essential supplies caused immense suffering to the civilian population in the north (UN Human Rights Commission 1987a). In response, the Commission adopted a resolution calling on Sri Lanka to cooperate with the International Committee of the Red Cross (ICRC) in the promotion of international humanitarian law, and urged the government to take up the ICRC's offer of services to protect humanitarian standards, including assistance and protection of victims of all affected parties (UN Human Rights Commission 1987b). However, restrictions were placed on the flow of humanitarian aid and continue to hamper the humanitarian response. In fact, according to the Relief and Rehabilitation Network the single most important impediment to effective humanitarian co-ordination was the Sri Lankan government, and particularly the military, which retained final authority and excluded other agencies from their decisions (Van Brabant 1997).

Box 6 Examples of government restrictions on materials to northern Sri Lanka, 2001
(For a comprehensive list of banned items see Appendix 1)

- All medicines
- Surgical equipment
- Dressings
- Sanitary pads
- Batteries (for example for torch-lights)

Source: Personal communication and Virakesari (Sri Lanka newspaper), 4 and 11 March 2001

The government introduced the Emergency Restriction of Transport of Articles Regulations in 1991, banning the transport of more than 40 commodities to the north including medicines, surgical instruments, bandages, fertilizers and fuel (SLG 1991; BRC 2001b). Although the materials were not listed, the Defense Ministry would without warning impose restrictions on other items such as bicycles and matches. The military also imposed severe restrictions on the movement of goods to LTTE-held territory in the east (BRC 1999d).

The imposition of restrictions on the transport of various items by government authorities continued (L & ST 2000), and in 1998 Sri Lankan human rights NGOs reported that the health situation in LTTE-held territory remained largely unimproved. In 1999 it was reported that the embargo aggravated the shortage of medical supplies and contributed to an already serious deterioration in the quality and quantity of health care (US State Department 2000). The government introduced further regulations and imposed further restrictions in 2001, including on fuel, fertilizer, cement and motor vehicle spare parts, as shown in Box 6 (SLG 2001b). Again, restrictions were placed on many materials that were not included in the regulations. The blockade inflicted severe hardship and affected health, industry, education, fishing and infrastructure – almost certainly resulting in avoidable deaths, including of many children.

The emergency regulations lapsed on 6 July 2001 when Parliament was prorogued, but further regulations re-establishing prohibited and restricted zones were immediately introduced under the Prevention of Terrorism Act. The Prohibited Zone encompassed the entire North-East, from Hambantota in the south through Trincomalee and Jaffna to Puttlam in the west, and forbade entry without a permit (SLG 2001c). These restrictions were reinforced by new regulations introduced after the ceasefire agreement (SLG 2002a). Although fishing is permitted in several places, coastal areas a mile either side of and two miles out to sea from a military base became restricted zones. Because of the high number of military bases, a large part of the Jaffna coastline fall within the zones, thus placing severe restrictions on fishing (Good 2003).

Government restrictions particularly affect LTTE-controlled areas. Nevertheless, health services have been delivered as efficiently as possible considering limited resources (WHO 2002). However the recent crisis has led to a drastic reduction in the availability of health-related resources.

Box 7 Violations of human rights and humanitarian law

There are several serious allegations and significant recognition of the failure of the government of Sri Lanka and its officials, officers, and agents to provide adequate and available food to populations in northern regions, including allegations that crops have been intentionally destroyed. There are also allegations that these failures are often deliberate: that the failure to provide adequate food is used as a political tactic or weapon of war against noncombatants in the northern regions for various purposes.

Serious violations of basic human rights and humanitarian law occur in Sri Lanka when food, medicine, and medical supplies are used as political weapons. Those least able to cope, especially children, are the primary victims of such criminal tactics.

Source: Paust 1998

In the 1990s, the A9 Kandy-Jaffna road linking the southern areas of Sri Lanka with Mullaitivu, Kilinochchi and Jaffna districts had been closed to general traffic. It was reopened on 15 February 2002 in the run-up to the ceasefire agreement but only between 7am and 5pm, a limitation which restricted economic revival of the north.

Following the intensification of fighting in August 2006, the government took several measures that resulted in further adverse effects for the civilian population. The government closed the A9 road again on 11 August 2006, preventing transport of essential materials and humanitarian aid. Its determination to keep the road closed has been described as part of its strategy to isolate the LTTE (Perera 2006). However this closure continues to have dire consequences for the civilian population.

A curfew was imposed in the Jaffna peninsula on 11 August 2006, and lifted for 2 hours only after 14 August. Later, an 11-hour nightly curfew between 6pm and 5am was introduced which has affected employment, education and people's freedom of movement. The night curfew isstill in force. The following entry points into the LTTE-controlled area of Paduvankarai in Batticaloa were closed on 12 August 2006: crossing points for boats at Kinnayady and Santhiveli, ferry services at Manmunai and Ambilanthurai, bridges at Kiran, Vavunathivu, Chenkalady and Paddiruppu, and crossing points for road vehicles at Kavathaimunai and Vaharai.

According to the UN, restrictions on the transport of construction materials, and on the movement of civilian, UN and NGO vehicles in parts of the north, means it is difficult to access certain areas, and this hampers recovery and has created shortages of drugs in local hospitals and clinics (UNOCHA 2006). Conflict, displacement and restrictions on the delivery of humanitarian aid have increased vulnerability to malnutrition and disease and many health facilities have been damaged or destroyed. The Watch List on Children and Armed Conflict (2008) says that the "ongoing armed conflict and access restrictions have prevented people in conflict-affected areas from accessing life-saving medical care, and children in particular suffer under these conditions". The World Food Programme warned of an emerging humanitarian emergency in Jaffna and Batticaloa and an acute food and livelihoods crisis in five other districts (WFP 2007a).

4.2 Restrictions on freedom of movement
Surveillance, Territorial, Prohibited and Security Zones: effects on freedom of movement, livelihoods, humanitarian assistance and health

The right to freedom of movement guaranteed by the Sri Lankan constitution has been severely curtailed for the Tamil population, particularly in the North-East. Checkpoints, restricted zones, military camps and prohibited areas have affected all aspects of life and eroded rights, including the right to health.

Prohibited zones and high security zones

Since the 1980s, under the Emergency Regulations (ER) and the Prevention of Terrorism

Act (PTA), the government has designated areas as prohibited zones and surveillance zones (demarcated at sea and along the adjoining coastline) and security zones and high security zones (demarcated on land) (Institute of Peace and Conflict Studies 2007). These zones have had a huge impact on economic, social and cultural life and health.

The Surveillance Zone, Territorial Zone, Prohibited Zone and Security Zone established in 1984 affected 200,000 fishermen and dependents in the region and led to the destitution of many families (Vije 1986). All forests, sanctuaries and national parks were made 'no-go' areas in 1985 and areas up to 1000m around all the camps of the security forces were declared security zones in 1986. The Territorial Zone was extended along the Eastern Province in 1986.

In the 1990s the government imposed further restrictions, particularly on the freedom of movement, targeting the entire Tamil population including in Colombo. Tamils were required to register with the police, providing family details, and to obtain permits to travel. ERs were issued in 1992 and 1993 re-establishing prohibited zones (SLG 1992, 1993a). Under a further ER in 1993, the Prohibited Zone was extended to include the Sri Lankan territorial waters of the five northern districts, and vehicles were forbidden without written permission (SLG 1993c). Another ER banned all boats in the northern sea between Mannar on the western coast and Trincomalee on the eastern coast (SLG 1993b). The livelihoods of nearly 100,000 fisher families were affected (BRC 1993b)

Table 6 The impact of High Security Zones

	Amparai	Batticaloa	Trincomalee	Vavuniya	Mullaitivu	Mannar	Jaffna	Total
Extent of HSZs (acres)	260	700	200	1,000	16,800	1,360	3,800	24,120
Number of houses in HSZs	72	399	305	1,505	1,004	50	28,830	32,165
Farmland made inaccessible by HSZs (acres)	40	86	50	106	16,711	42	12,929	29,964
Coastline made inaccessible by HSZs (km)	1	1	20	21	19	24	80	166
Schools within HSZs unable to function	-	1	-	21	4	7	35	68
Places of worship made inaccessible by HSZs	-	-	-	22	-	2	80	104
Public places made inaccessible by HSZs*	4	31	-	49	14	4	32	134

Humanitarian assistance to civilians in Mullaitivu and Kilinochchi districts came to a near standstill after the closing of the Pappamoddai checkpoint in 1999 which in effect banned movement across the forward defence lines (Human Rights Watch 1999a). International humanitarian agencies operating in the area reported that thousands of civilians had been trapped without access to assistance on both sides of the checkpoint, families were separated and no food rations were delivered for five weeks. Civilians faced increasing difficulties obtaining food, which was becoming increasingly expensive and beyond the reach of most families. There was a risk of serious health problems particularly for children.

Security zones

The restrictions continued in the new millennium. Tamils were required to obtain police passes in order to move freely in the North-East region, and were often harassed at checkpoints around the country (US State Department 2001). Tamil civilians were unable to reach their places of work, attend schools or seek urgent health care (HRW 2001). In the Jaffna peninsula 18 high security zones remain to this day and cover approximately 190 sq. km. (IPCS 2007). Civilians have been forcibly evicted from the zones and have no access to their homes, land and marine resources. Many IDPs are unable to return because their homes lie within the zones, which cover a fifth of the Jaffna peninsula, and zones in the North-East have displaced over 120,000 people (UN Special Representative 2008). The entire population of the Jaffna peninsula is affected by restrictions, and freedom of movement is heavily constrained by numerous checkpoints manned by the armed forces (MSF 2008). Obtaining visas and official authorizations for MSF international field staff take up to eight weeks, due to recent restrictions that greatly hindered its ability to provide assistance. The Sri Lankan government issued orders in September 2008 requiring some 100,000 Tamils who had fled from the five northern districts and were living in Colombo to register with the police (Internal Displacement Monitoring Centre 2008b).

Graph 2 Impact of High Security Zones

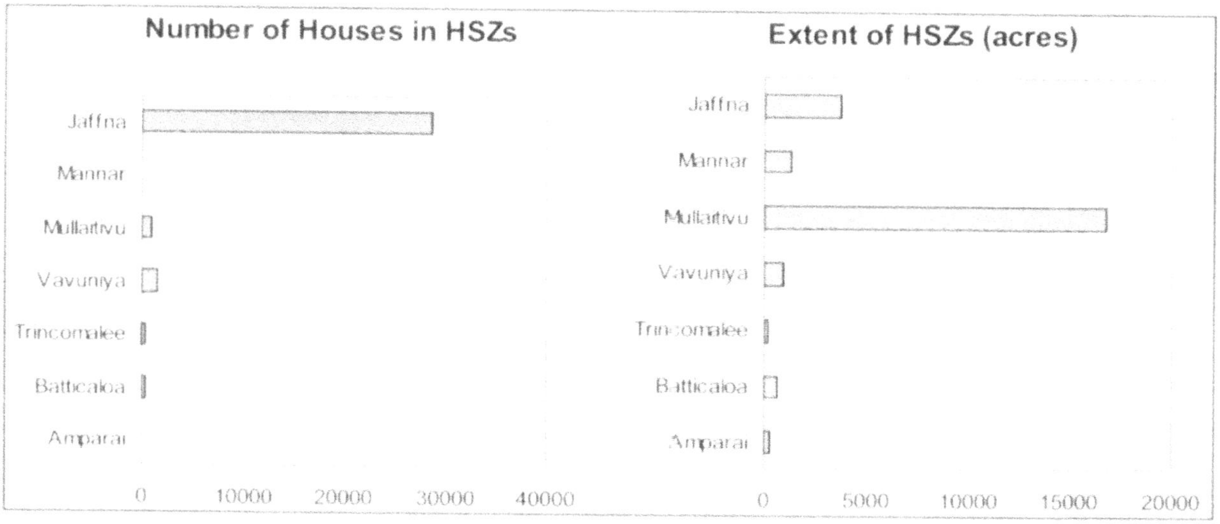

Note: * This includes government departments, other government and local government buildings, private companies, cooperative stores, markets, community halls, railway stations, fuel stations, banks, rice mills, libraries, dispensaries, schools, temples and churches.

Travel permits

The crossing point into the northern LTTE-controlled territory lies at Omanthai, three miles north of Vavuniya town. The Sri Lankan military maintains a checkpoint at Omanthai that was operational throughout the conflict of the 1990s. Throughout the 1990s, even after the army had captured parts of the Jaffna peninsula in 1995 and 1996, Tamils travelling to Jaffna were required to obtain permits from the Defence Ministry; a process that could take more than three months. As the A-9 road was closed this meant thousands of people often waited in Trincomalee to travel by ship to Jaffna. Jaffna residents were required to apply to the army's civil administration office to travel outside the peninsula. This procedure also took a long time, with thousands of people waiting for permits at any given time. People in the Vanni were required to obtain permits from the LTTE, and, before 2001, those entering the Vanni needed permits from the army headquarters in Vavuniya town; subsequently the government ordered that travel permits to the Vanni should be obtained from the Defence Ministry in Colombo. IDPs in camps in Vavuniya were required to obtain permits just to visit the town (BRC 2001b; L & ST 1995, 1998, 2001).

The Representative of the UN Secretary-General on the Human Rights of Internally Displaced Persons acknowledged that the Sri Lankan state faced legitimate and serious security concerns. But he also said the pervasive military presence and strict procedures had severely restricted movement of IDPs and returnees and undermined their sense of security (UN Representative 2008).

4.3 Food shortages

Inadequate supplies and security effects on agriculture and fishing; food security and general rations, decreasing supplies; blockades and price increases; humanitarian emergency

From 1990, transport difficulties and government restrictions on essential items and fishing drastically reduced food supplies. Continuing disruption of electricity supplies and shortages of fertilizers, implements, equipment, insecticides and fuel had a severe impact on food production within the region, causing steep price rises.

The region received less than a third of its relief requirements in 1991. Jaffna district received 7233 tonnes of food and other relief materials in January and February, compiling 25% of basic needs; however it needed 300,000 litres of kerosene and 200,000 litres of diesel to bring home the major Maha (November–March rice cultivation season) rice harvest, and supplies of these items were drastically cut (BRC 1991c). In 1993, the military's Joint Operations Command informed the Jaffna Government Agent that the supply of kerosene would be reduced from 5000 to 1500 barrels and each family in the peninsula would receive only one litre of kerosene per month. Since kerosene is the primary source of energy, for example, for light and cooking, this restriction has affected daily activities and furthermore has drastically curtailed agricultural activity (BRC 1993a).

Following an LTTE attack on the navy, the government banned boats in the northern sea between Mannar and Trincomalee in 1993, and extended the Prohibited Zone to the Sri Lankan territorial waters of the five northern districts so vessels were forbidden to enter these areas without written permission (SLG 1993c). These measures reduced the incomes of 100,000 families who depended on fishing for their livelihoods (BRC 1993b).

The Essential Services Commissioner supplied only 13% of food requirements to Jaffna district in 1990; this increased to 57% in 1993, but fell to 27% the following year. In 1990 it provided only 19% of the milk powder needed for Jaffna children, and in 1994 this fell to just 4%. Table 7 shows the food supplied in the 1990-1994 period.

Table 7 Food requirements and food supplied by the Essential Services Commissioner by ship to Jaffna district, 1990-1994

Item	Annual need	Stocks received in Jaffna from the Essential Services Commissioner*									
		1990	%	1991	%	1992	%	1993	%	1994	%
Rice	82,500	8,170	10	30,145	37	20,077	24	33,200	40	9,049	11
Flour	29,700	5,977	20	26,773	90	30,012	101	34,405	116	23,418	79
Sugar	16,144	3,371	21	6,940	43	9,677	60	11,201	69	5,651	35
Lentils	12,375	1,287	10	1,822	15	920	7	2,353	19	1,259	10
Milk powder	3,000	560	19	1,889	63	969	32	636	21	120	4
Total	143,719	19,365	13	67,569	47	61,655	43	81,795	57	39,497	27

Note: * In tonnes

Source: 'Special report on the situation in the Jaffna District' by K Manickavasagar, Jaffna Government Agent, in Victims of war in Sri Lanka: a quest for health consensus - Medical Institute of Tamils (UK), Tamil Information Centre (UK) and Tamil Refugee Relief Organization (US) (1995).

Following a joint mission in 1996, World Food Programme (WFP) and Food and Agricultural Organization (FAO) officials said that 510,000 people affected by displacement and drought were not receiving sufficient food aid. They also said military operations were preventing these people from cultivating their fields, and noted that difficulties and delays caused by military checkpoints were resulting in a significant increase in transport costs (FAO 1997). In 1997, the government replaced cash payments to refugees with dry rations, reducing the relief to larger families (BRC 1997a). When the army launched Operation Certain Victory on 13 May 1997 to open a land route to Jaffna through the Vanni, transport across the Thandikulam checkpoint was suspended, creating new food and medicine shortages (BRC 1997b). Four days earlier, the Essential Services Commissioner ordered an arbitrary reduction in the number of people receiving food aid from 420,000 to 185,000 (BRC 1997c). The army halted all bus services to the LTTE-controlled Vaharai, in the Eastern Province, in August 1997 to prevent people taking food and fuel into the area (BRC 1997f).

The 1997 report of the Foodfirst Information and Action Network International to the 17th session of the UN Committee on Economic Social and Cultural Rights said that the government's Triposha (nutritional food supplement) programme for children had not reached the North-East for two years (BRC 1997g). The committee expressed grave concern in 1998 regarding the situation of "an estimated 800,000 persons displaced because of the armed conflict, many of whom have been living in temporary shelters for the past 15 years and who lack basic sanitation, education, food, clothing and health care". It was alarmed by an independent survey which estimated the incidence of undernourished women and children living in temporary shelters to be as high as 70%, and by reports that food assistance often did not reach the intended beneficiaries UN Committee on Economic Social and Cultural Rights 1998).

In January 1998, the Vavuniya Government Agent reported that dry rations from the government were sufficient to supply only 270,000 people, whereas there were an estimated 440,000 IDPs in the Vanni (BRC 1998a). The government nevertheless decided to make significant cuts in food rations (US State Department 2000), announcing that from 1 July 1998 food aid would be cut by 40% in Jaffna, 20% in Kilinochchi and Mullaitivu and 15% in Mannar and Vavuniya. However, in July 1998 the Essential Services Commissioner cut the food supply to the Vanni by 55% and the government agents could only provide food to 180,000 people (BRC 1998b). The number of families receiving food aid was thus reduced arbitrarily to 55,500 from 81,200 (BRC 1998c).

As the food crisis continued, the Jaffna NGO Consortium appealed to the UN Secretary General (BRC 1999e). In November 1998 the Vanni government agents reported that 15,400 barrels of kerosene were needed in the first four months of 1999 to cultivate over 100,000 acres of land, but the the Defense Ministry had allowed permits for only 325 barrels (BRC 1998d). On 5 November 1998 the military banned fishing in the Jaffna lagoon; fishermen were allowed to fish only between 5.30am and 3.30pm, a restriction soon extended to the whole of the Jaffna peninsula (BRC 1998e). The Vavuniya Government Agent reported in May 1999 that 315 lorry loads of food, the first due to be delivered to the Vanni since March 1999, had been stopped after the military launched Operation Battle Cry I (BRC 1999a). The food shortage in the Vanni became more acute with the launch of Operation Battle Cry IV in June 1999, which disrupted supplies through the checkpoint at Pappamoddai along the north-western coast. The checkpoint was closed on 26 June 1999. Human Rights Watch expressed concern that conditions for civilians trapped in the north, including hundreds of thousands of IDPs, had become critical after the only supply route to the Vanni closed; they were without adequate food, medical care and other humanitarian assistance for weeks; and the risk of acute malnutrition in children was growing (HRW 1999b).

After six weeks of a full blockade, food lorries were permitted into the Vanni following an agreement between the government and the LTTE negotiated by the International Committee of the Red Cross (BRC 1999c). The food supply to the Vanni was cut off when the LTTE launched Operation Unceasing Waves on 2 November 1999. From 9 December 1999 the Defense Ministry permitted 60 lorry loads of food per week, but government agents said 515 additional lorry loads were needed (BRC 1999f). The Defence Ministry ordered a 30% cut in the supply of food to Mullaitivu and Kilinochchi from 1 January 2000 (BRC 2000a). On 15 February 2002, a week before the signing of the ceasefire agreement, the government opened the A-9 road and food was allowed into the north, while traffic was also allowed into LTTE-controlled areas in the east. However, haggling between the military and LTTE continued during the ceasefire period, and military and security issues rather than the people's welfare became the primary focus during negotiations.

After fighting resumed in Trincomalee, the government closed the A-9 Kandy-Jaffna road in August 2006 and closed the entry points to LTTE-controlled areas in Batticaloa. This resulted in shortages of essential goods, including milk food for children in the LTTE-controlled areas of the North-East and the army-controlled areas of the Jaffna peninsula. Jaffna's population needed 11,000 tonnes of food per month including rice, wheat flour, sugar, lentils and milk food, but between 22 August 2006 and 4 November 2006 government ships supplied only 19,250 tonnes (58%) (TIC 2006). An 11-hour nightly curfew between 6pm and 5am affected employment, livelihoods such as fishing, business, education and the movement of patients for emergency treatment.

The restrictions drove up the prices of essential commodities, some by as much as tenfold in comparison with those in other regions. Bakeries were unable to make bread and other food because they had no wheat flour. Many businesses were forced to close. The lack of food badly affected vulnerable groups such as the elderly, the disabled, widows, people traumatized by the war and the tsunami, IDPs and children (Human Development Centre 2006, TIC 2006). Although the government continued to bring in supplies by ship to the army-controlled areas of Jaffna and set up a rationing system, there were concerns about shortages of flour, rice, sugar and lentils (UNICEF 2006b).

In 2007, the WFP placed Kilinochchi, Mullaitivu, Trincomalee, Mannar and parts of Vavuniya in the Integrated Food Security and Humanitarian Phase Classification category of 'Acute Food and Livelihood Crisis' owing to the armed conflict and the government-imposed embargo on fuel, agricultural and construction materials. This was defined by six key outcome indicators: under-five mortality; crude mortality; stunting; wasting; water/sanitation; and livelihood assets (female literacy, access to health facilities, road access, banks). Other indicators were also used to give a more comprehensive picture: poverty, infant mortality, under-nutrition, real wages, rice production and productivity growth, rice self-sufficiency, and physical access to markets.

By 2007, Jaffna and Batticaloa districts, classified as a 'humanitarian emergency', were facing a widespread high-intensity conflict with thousands of IDPs, collapsing markets, increasing malnutrition and great income losses (WFP 2007b). Some 800,000 people were in need of life-saving humanitarian emergency assistance in Jaffna and Batticaloa. According to the WFP, "these include not only the IDPs but those households that were living below the poverty line prior to the conflict and whose access to food has become unsustainable due to the conflict. Another 900,000 need support with livelihood protection as their coping strategies are depleting in Kilinochchi, Mannar, Mullaitivu, Vavuniya and Trincomalee" (WFP 2007a).

In April 2008, UN food experts warned that a poor rice harvest, rising global food prices and the enduring conflict were increasing food insecurity for hundreds of thousands of Sri Lankans. Jean-Yves Lequime, WFP deputy head in Sri Lanka, said the highest rates of under-nutrition were in the North-East as well as parts of the dry zone: these areas had "very high under-nutrition rates, poor education levels and poor sanitation, all of which contribute to under-nutrition" (UNOCHA 2008c).

4.4 Impact on agriculture, fishing and industry

Effects of conflict on falling production; effects for agriculture, animal husbandry and industry

Before the war the North-East of the country produced substantial quantities of food and other agricultural products, including rice, onions, green chillies and tobacco (see box 8). Produce from these areas also supplied southern areas. Since the war began, agricultural, industrial, fishing and commercial activities have been drastically affected by various factors including:

> bombing, landmines and unexploded ordnance;
> government restrictions on fuel, fertilizers, pest-control chemicals,
> agricultural implements, equipment and fishing;
> security measures such as high security zones and
> problems with marketing, transport and distribution.

With the resumption of war and increased government restrictions, agriculture has again been badly affected and production is expected to decline.

Bombing and mines have killed a large number of farm animals, and the large-scale displacement of people means animal husbandry has become impossible in some areas. Between 1981 and 2000, the number of farm animals decreased from 1,978,000 to 1,656,000 with a consequent fall in milk, meat and egg production (ADB et al 2003). The number of goats in the north was a third of the national total in 1980, but fell to a quarter in 1990 and 15% in 2000. The number of sheep was 72% of the national total in 1980, but declined to 65% in 1990 and 61% in 2000. The region contributed 13% of the country's egg output in 1980, but this had declined to 9% in 1990 and 2000. It increased during the ceasefire period and was 13% in 2005 (Sarvananthan 2007).

Due to the declaration of security zones and other restrictions, whole communities of fishermen cannot access the sea, or cannot fish at night when catches are best (UN Special Representative 2008). The enormous impact of security restrictions on fishing was evident by the improvement in catch after the ceasefire in 2001

Graph 3 Contrbution of North-East to total fish catch (1980-2005)

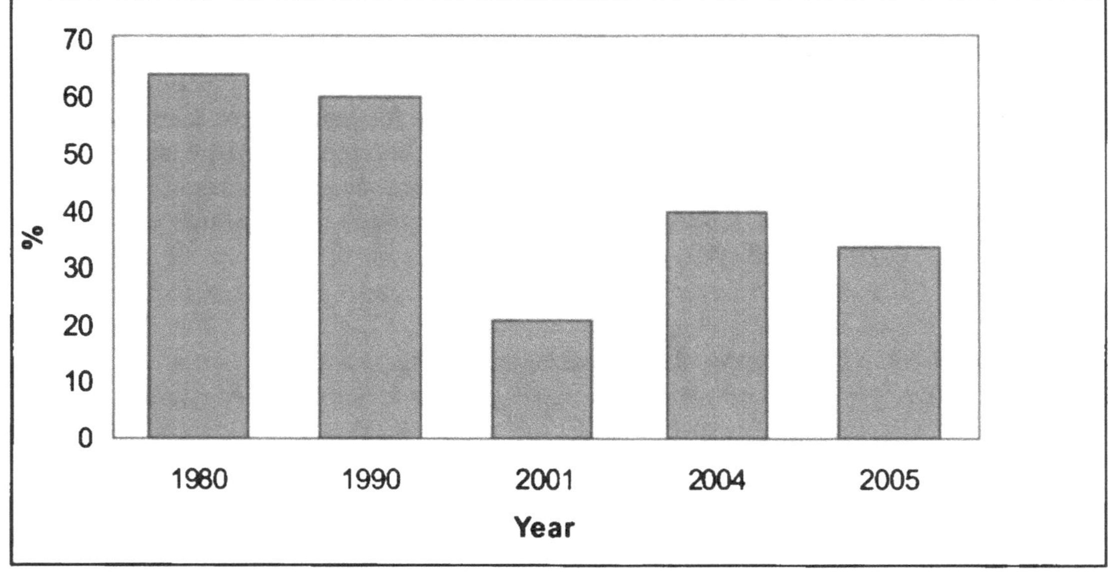

Source: Sarvanathan (2007)

The removal of security restrictions in most parts of the north during the ceasefire has been an enormous help to the fisheries industry, although in 2005 the catch declined once again due to the tsunami. This is illustrated by the fall in the contribution by the North-East to the national fish industry, as shown by Graph 3, and the absolute numbers of fish catch in tonnes has fallen drastically since 1980 for the North-East.

Another importmant industry for the Sri Lankan economy as a whole is the tourist industry which is one of the biggest foreign exchange earners and accounts for over 10% of gross domestic product (GDP) (IMF 2008a). For the period 1989-2002 net tourism revenues averaged LKR1,668m, but for the period 2003-2005 (there is no more up-to-date data available) revenues increased almost 10-fold to LKR15,826m (IMF 2008a).

After independence, the state established just three major state-owned industries   a paper factory at Valaichenai in Batticaloa, a chemical factory at Paranthan in Kilinochchi, and a cement factory at Kankesanthurai in Jaffna. In the early 1980s these factories produced 100,000 tonnes of paper, 3900 tonnes of chemicals and 500,000 tonnes of cement. The total number of employees in these industries dropped from 50,400 in 1983 to 44,700 in 2003, while nationally the number of employees increased by 65% during the same period (Sarvananthan 2007). These factories never achieved optimum productivity, and Valaichenai paper factory is the only remaining operating factory.

The consequence of the declines in major industrial and agricultural activities is a sharp fall in overall output and incomes in the region. For 2006, IMF reports that the north and east contributed just 16% of the country's growth (see Table 8). However, there is a dearth of regional statistics for in-depth analysis. GDP measures the overall output of the economy and analysing this data for the period 1989-2001, real GDP growth averaged 5.8% (IMF 2008b). During the period of the ceasefire 2002-2007, growth was 6.0% per annum. This difference may not seem substantial but it is partly underestimated by the impact of the tsunami in 2004, which clearly depressed economic activity. Furthermore, examination of the impact on the North-East would show more marked effects of the confict. Analysis of national incomes clearly shows significant differences in GDP per capita in dollar current prices (which takes into account population differences but again does not adjust for the tsunami). It shows average growth of 9.7% per annum for the period 1989 to 2001, but a more impressive growth of 17.6% per annum between 2002 and 2007(IMF 2008b).

Box 8 Trends in crop production

Rice

In the North-East, total crops exceeded 800,000 tonnes in 1982 but slumped to less than 450,000 tonnes in 2001 (ADB et al 2003). The region accounted for 33% of the country's rice production in 1980, but by 2000 this had fallen to 24%. During the ceasefire, rice production increased and the contribution of the region was 30%, and by 2004 it was 36%.

Onions

The region accounted for almost two-thirds of onion production in 1980 and 1990, but production fell to 57% of the national total in 2000, to less than 33% in 2001-2003, and to 23% in 2005. In 1980, the Northern Province produced more than 31,000 tonnes of onions, and in 1990 32,000 tonnes, but by 2000 production had fallen to 15,700 tonnes. The Eastern Province accounted for 7% of the national onion production in 1980 and 1990. This had increased to 16% in 2000. During the period 2001-2003 the onion production had fallen to 8% of the total national production and to nearly 3% in 2005 (Sarvananthan 2007).

Chillis

Green chilli production was 13,000 tonnes in 1980 and 1990, but dropped to 4,300 tonnes in 2000. Chilli production increased during the ceasefire to 6500 tonnes between 2001 and 2005, but as a share of national output dropped from 25% in 1980 to 13% in 1990 and to 8% in 2000. After an increase of 15% in 2004, it declined again to 11% in 2005 (Sarvananthan 2007).

4.5 **Damage to Infrastructure**
Conflict damage to public health infrastructure: roads and communications

Another consequence of the war has been the damage to the infrastructure of the region, including water, electricity, roads, and telecommunications. Such infrastructure is essential for economic growth and poverty alleviation. It is one of the principal causes of regional inequalities in the country according to regular IMF staff reports affecting both the health and labour productivity of the local population (IMF 2007).

The Central Bank of Sri Lanka report that 91% of the households in the Northern Province and 92% in the Eastern Province had access to safe drinking water in 2003-2004, below the national average of nearly 94%, though this survey did not include the poor North-East districts of Kilinochchi, Mannar and Mullaitivu (SLG 2004). Furthermore, many families have lived in refugee camps for years in appalling conditions, and even more continue to live with friends or relatives, with the attendant pressures on facilities and resources. A higher percentage of households in the region have access to safe drinking water than in some other provinces only because of the interventions of international agencies (WHO 2002). The Northern and Eastern provinces had the lowest share of households with electricity in 1983 as well as in 2005. Only 5% of the national total of households with electricity in 1983 were in the Northern Province and only 6% were in the Eastern Province. In 2005, only 4% of households with electricity were in the Northern Province and 6% in the Eastern Province (WHO 2006).

Roads are important for access to markets and mobility. The destruction of roads in the war, poor maintenance and neglect in planning new roads for nearly three decades has resulted in the lowest road density (length of roads per sq. km.) in the North-East. The tsunami also destroyed roads in the region. In 2005, the road density in the Northern Province was 0.29 km/sq km and in the Eastern Province 0.28 km/sq km (WHO 2006). The government has restricted telephone lines to the region and many lines were destroyed in the war. The military has prohibited the use of mobile phones in many areas. In 2005, land telephone density in the Northern Province was just two telephones per 100 people, and the density in the Eastern Province was three per 100 persons, the lowest in the country (WHO 2006). National statistics give a figure of seven for the country as a whole (rising to sixteen by the third quarter of 2008).

Table 8 Regional contributions to growth, 2006

Province	Share of GDP (%)
West and Northwest	59.4
South and Central	24.3
North and East	16.3
National (Total)	100

Source: Central Bank of Sri Lanka in IMF 2007

5 Violence against civilians

5.1 Security force attacks
Deaths due to military actors; lack of accountability

The Sri Lankan security forces have killed thousands of civilians in the North-East. Bombing raids by the air force have caused high levels of death and destruction since 1990, damaging health institutions, schools and places of worship. In September 1990, 117 people were rounded up and shot in the Sathurukondan army camp in Batticaloa (BRC 1990b). The army massacred 180 Tamil civilians, many of them women and children, at Kokkaddicholai in June 1991 (BRC 1991d). Following the deaths of military commanders in Jaffna on 8 August 1992, the army raided Mahilanthanai village and killed 35 Tamil civilians (INFORM 1993). The air force bombed Jaffna town on 5 December 1993, killing 43 civilians and wounding 70 (BRC 1993c). On 9 July 1995, 65 civilians were killed when the air force bombed a church in Jaffna; the government censured the International Committee of the Red Cross for releasing information about the killings (BRC 1995a).

Hours after the government announced the introduction of military censorship in September 1995, the air force bombed a Nagarcoil schoolyard where 750 children were having their lunch break, killing 34 and seriously injuring 150. Two MSF surgeons worked through the night at Manthikai hospital in Point Pedro, carrying out 22 amputations (BRC 1995b). An army shell hit Akkarayankulam hospital staff residences in Kilinochchi on 15 July 1997, killing four people and wounding six (BRC 1997d). Soldiers killed 24 Tamil civilians at Kumarapuram on 11 February 1996 (AI 1996). On 15 August 1997, the air force killed six Tamil refugees and wounded seventeen others at Vavunikulam (BRC 1997e). After the LTTE killed a soldier on 19 August 1999, soldiers ran riot shooting and injuring fourteen Tamil civilians and burning eight houses in Sunny village on the island of Mannar (BRC 1999b). On 17 May 2000, security forces shot dead nine orphan children and wounded 20 others in Batticaloa town (BRC 2000b). The air force bombed several villages in Kilinochchi on 21 March 2001, killing thirteen civilians and wounding 24 (BRC 2001a). On 9 March 2002, the Special Task Force fired on demonstrators in Kanchikudichcharu, killing seven Tamil civilians and injuring thirteen (BRC 2002). Twelve Tamil civilians were massacred by the navy on 13 June 2006 at Allaipiddy on Kayts island (AI 2006). On 14 August 2006, the air force bombed a children's centre in Mullaitivu, killing 60 children and injuring 150 (UNICEF 2006a).

No proper enquiries have been conducted into these and hundreds of other killings carried out by the security forces. Where investigations have been initiated, they have reached no conclusions and victims' families have not been compensated.

5.2 Torture
Institutional abuse; methods used; medical complicity; lack of available forensic skills; international condemnation

Torture by the security forces has continued for several decades and is widespread, systematic, well known and proven to be institutionalized, despite international condemnation. Amnesty International and other agencies recorded over 120,000 Tamil arrests between 1990 and 2001, and thousands more have since been arrested (see AI annual reports 1990-2001, and US State Department country reports 1990-2001). Most arrests are arbitrary, carried out in round-ups, and many people are detained illegally. A large number of these people have suffered torture or degrading treatment, both physical and mental, carried out by armed forces, paramilitary groups and police in military camps and police stations. There are also allegations of sexual violence and abuse of women and children in custody, and intimidation of and threats against those reporting torture. There are no effective witness and victim protection mechanisms in cases of torture. According to the victims, detention centres have special rooms, equipment and devices for the purpose of torture. The UK's Medical Foundation for the Care of Victims of Torture found that Tamils had suffered beatings, suspension, semi-suffocation, verbal abuse, cuts from knives and bayonets, burns from hot metal and cigarettes, and severe and prolonged sexual abuse; all the victims studied reported physical problems, and about 40% reported continuing psychological symptoms (Medical Foundation for the Care of Victims of Torture 2000).

Box 9 UN condemns torture in Sri Lanka

The UN Committee against Torture expressed its concern in 2005 as follows:

"Continued well-documented allegations of widespread torture and ill-treatment as well as disappearances, mainly committed by the State's police forces. It is also concerned that such violations by law enforcement officials are not investigated promptly and impartially by the State party's competent authorities.

Continued allegations of sexual violence and abuse of women and children in custody, including by law enforcement officials, as well as the lack of prompt and impartial investigations of these allegations.

Undue delay of trials, especially trials of people accused of torture.

Alleged reprisals, intimidation and threats against persons reporting acts of torture and ill-treatment as well as the lack of effective witness and victim protection mechanisms."

Source: UN Office of the High Commissioner for Human Rights 2005

The UN Special Rapporteur on Torture, during his visit in 2007, came across complaints about a broad variety of torture methods, some extremely brutal. Many allegations were corroborated by forensic evidence. He concluded that torture had become routine in counter-terrorism operations by police and armed forces, noting the considerable number of clearly established cases of torture carried out by the Terrorist Investigation Division and other security forces, and their attempts to hide evidence and obstruct his investigations (UN Special Rapporteur 2008). The methods reported included beating with various weapons, beating on the soles of the feet (falaqa), blows to the ears (telephono), positional abuse when handcuffed or bound, suspension in various positions, including strappado, 'butchery', 'reversed butchery' and 'parrot's perch' (dharma chakara), burning with metal objects and cigarettes, asphyxiation with plastic bags with chilli pepper or gasoline and various forms of genital torture. The detention facility in Boossa used the widest range of methods. The Special Rapporteur was shocked by the torture of suspected LTTE members, such as burning with soldering irons and suspension by the thumbs.

Sri Lankan and other human rights agencies have recorded a variety of torture methods used by Sri Lankan security forces (TIC 2008b):

- beating with plastic pipes filled with cement, batons, belts or chains,
- stamping while wearing boots,
- hanging by the legs and beating all parts of the body,
- burning with cigarettes,
- suffocating by covering the head with plastic bags soaked in petrol,
- beating on the soles of the feet,
- inserting bottles, batons or barbed wire into the rectum,
- applying chilli powder or other material to sensitive parts of the body,
- detention in a dark room,
- repeated kicking and punching,
- tying to a chair and beating,
- tying hands together and hanging from a pole,
- giving electric shocks,
- repeatedly smashing the head against a wall,
- inserting needles into fingernails and other parts of the body,
- injecting liquids into various parts of the body,
- sleep deprivation and sexual abuse.

Tamil victims are almost always forced to sign a confession under torture or threat of torture, and these confessions are used in evidence against them in court. Provisions in the Prevention of Terrorism Act and Emergency Regulations that allow confessions as substantive evidence in court encourage torture (UN Special Rapporteur 2008).

Involvement of doctors in torture

Many victims allege that doctors were present during their torture in detention centres. Doctors examining victims of severe torture may be persuaded by police or military officers to exclude evidence of torture from their reports, or to refrain from reporting it to higher authorities (Jayasekera 1999). Police and security forces can pressurize health professionals who work in conflict areas (International Rehabilitation Council for Torture Victims 2004). The Sri Lanka Medical Council has failed to carry out proper investigations into these long-standing allegations. Human Rights Watch has highlighted the pressure put on doctors to cover up evidence of gang rape and sexual torture, for example bypolice and naval personnel of two women arrested by anti-subversion police in Mannar in March 2002. The district medical officer's initial report said there were no signs of mistreatment, but after the women's complaints were made public, examination by a second doctor concluded that the women had indeed been tortured and raped (HRW 2002).

There are about 27 forensic medicine specialists in Sri Lanka, many of whom are in major cities and university departments. In addition, over 200 medical doctors in state hospitals examine torture victims, but are not trained in forensic medical evaluation. Psychological evaluations are rarely performed, and psychiatrists are rarely involved in preparing forensic reports when there is a referral by the courts (HRW 2002).

Forensic examination of torture victims

The UN Special Rapporteur on Torture found that victims of torture were usually accompanied to a Judicial Medical Officer by the same police officers responsible for the alleged torture or ill-treatment. Medical examinations frequently take place in the presence of the perpetrators, or are carried out by junior doctors with little experience in the documentation of injuries. The independence of the examination for physical evidence of torture is thus compromised. Further, access to a Judicial Medical Officer is not guaranteed and alleged victims are often examined by doctors with no qualification in forensic medicine. Detainees have reported that habeas corpus hearings before a magistrate involve no real opportunity to complain about police torture, as they are often escorted to court by the perpetrators, and that the magistrate does not inquire whether the suspect has been mistreated (UN Special Rapporteur 2008).

Prison medical staff told the Special Rapporteur that they regularly heard allegations of torture and other forms of ill-treatment by people transferred from police stations to prison. These complaints were often corroborated by physical evidence such as scars and haematomas. However, they only felt responsible for treating obvious wounds and did not take further action, such as reporting alleged abuse to the authorities or sending victims to a Judicial Medical Officer. The Rapporteur noted that restricted access to these officers resulted in loss of important medical evidence, which in turn impeded criminal proceedings against perpetrators. The absence of an obligation on law enforcement officials or judges to investigate cases of torture ex officio further aggravated the victims' plight (UN Special Rapporteur 2008).

5.3 Killings and death threats
Extra-judicial killings; frequency; lack of accountability

Amnesty International report 80,000 people have been killed in conflict-related deaths since 1983 (2008a), and this figure is widely cited by other agencies and the media. However, the most recent independent study using WHO world heath survey data suggests there were 220,000 conflict-related deaths between 1985 and 2002 (Obermeyer et al 2008). Over 2000 Tamils had probably already died in the Black July violence of 1983 (Tambiah 1986). There was clear evidence of complicity of government ministers and state officers, which probably explains why no investigation took place. No thorough investigations have been undertaken into the many massacres carried out by security forces. In addition, nearly 6000 people are reported to have died in the North-East since July 2006, including by extra-judicial executions. Following the escalation of war since early January according to Human Right Watch there were 7,000 casualties including 2,000 deaths (Human Rights Watch 2009). Responsibility for these deaths should be shared by the Sri Lankan security forces with the aligned non-state paramilitary groups and the LTTE.

The Special Rapporteur on Extra-judicial Executions says that almost none of the extrajudicial executions by the security forces have been effectively investigated and that the LTTE regularly issues unconvincing denials of responsibility for killings but fails to denounce any of those that suit their purposes (UN Special Rapporteur 2006). Many people have been abducted and murdered by so-called 'unidentified persons', and their bodies dumped in public places. Journalists, human rights defenders, NGO officials, government officials and Tamil members of parliament have received death threats from the military. Many of those threatened in Jaffna have taken refuge in the prison, where they are held alongside other prisoners. The military has also directly threatened members of the judiciary in the North-East, and judges in army-controlled areas are unable to perform their duties effectively.

5.4 Disappearances and abductions

Widespread disappearances; lack of official action; death squads; official implication and complicity

'Disappearances' are a widespread problem. Many people have 'disappeared' during cordon and search operations, at military checkpoints and during curfew hours. People living near military installations are vulnerable, while many who have gone to police stations to record witness statements have themselves been disappeared or killed. In some instances, several members of one family who made statements to the police have disappeared, indicating that the police are informing the military about witnesses and are involved in disappearances.

Four presidential commissions inquired into 37,662 of the 54,404 complaints of disappearances that took place between 1988 and 1995. They found evidence of disappearance in 21,115 cases and recorded the names of the security force personnel responsible, but no further action has been taken in any of these cases (UN Working Group 1999). No enquiries have been conducted into a further 16,742 cases. A new presidential commission headed by Justice N K Udalagama was appointed in 2006 to inquire into specific complaints of abductions, disappearances and unexplained killings. Experts from 11 countries were invited to observe and ensure that the commission's investigations were conducted in a transparent manner and in accordance with international standards. However, the International Independent Group of Eminent Persons (2007) found that the conduct of the presidential commission was inconsistent with international standards. The government has neither published the commission's reports nor acted on its recommendations, and the disappearances continue - after the army captured Jaffna in 1996, 765 people disappeared (AHRC 2000).

Hundreds of Tamils have been abducted in the North-East and Colombo, creating a climate of fear among the Tamil population and expatriate visitors. Over 100 Tamils have been abducted in Colombo and other southern areas since February 2006, including journalists, students and women. The bodies of twelve people were found later and the fate of 60 people is unknown. Sixteen people were released after paying huge ransoms; these monies are paid into named bank accounts, but the banks and police are unwilling to investigate contravention of the 2006 Prevention of Money Laundering Act 5. Members of organizations, parliamentarians and others who have attempted to investigate abductions have received death threats.

Of the 900 people who went missing in Jaffna between December 2005 and August 2007, 252 were traced - of whom 129 were found in security force detention (78 were released later). The security forces gave no information about arrest and detention to relatives or the Sri Lanka Human Rights Commission as required by presidential directives. Seventeen people who went missing were brought in vehicles by unidentified people and dropped off at various places, and thirteen bodies were found later. According to the list, 648 people are still missing; 194 of these were witnessed being abducted by the security forces (TIC 2008a).

Abductions are carried out in white vans without number plates, a hallmark of military death squads. They operate at night and during curfew hours and pass though military and police checkpoints without difficulty before and after the abductions, suggesting involvement or complicity of the security forces. Despite the appointment of the commissions, abductions have continued and not a single case has been resolved by the law enforcement agencies (AHRC 2006).

Sri Lanka had the highest number of disappearances in the world in 2007, according to the UN Working Group on Enforced Disappearances, which told the UN Human Rights Council that the Sri Lankan Army and the Criminal Investigation Department were allegedly responsible for a large number of disappearances. Other possible perpetrators include the Sri Lankan security forces and the police (UN Working Group 2008). The Working Group has called on the Sri Lankan government to stamp out the recent wave of disappearances, during which women and humanitarian aid workers have also gone missing (UN press release 2008).

The Working Group referred 107 cases to the Government as per standard procedure. Most took place between January 2006 and April 2007 and concerned men aged 20-35, although one case concerned a pregnant woman and two cases concerned minors. Seven cases concerned humanitarian aid workers, and another two cases concerned fishermen. The Sri Lankan Army, the police and the Criminal Investigation Department were allegedly responsible for most of these cases. The vast majority occurred in Colombo, although several occurred in Jaffna and Vavuniya.

5.5 Internally displaced persons

Large numbers displaced and left the country; vulnerability of IDPs; air strikes on civilians; government pressure on humanitarian agencies

Nearly a million people, 95% of them Tamil, were displaced in the North-East after fighting broke out in June 1990. Around 120,000 Tamils fled to India, increasing the Sri Lankan refugee population in the state of Tamil Nadu to 220,000 (BRC 1990a). Over 935,000 people had been displaced by July 1990 (BRC 2003). Since 1983, more than 400,000 Tamils have sought asylum in Europe and North America. In addition, more than 75,000 Muslims were forcibly evicted from the Northern Province by the LTTE in 1990 (BRC 1990c). Some IDPs were able to return home when a cessation of hostilities was announced in 1995, but fighting soon broke out again following the collapse of peace talks and the displacement continued. Over 200,000 people fled their homes in Jaffna when the army launched Operation Leap Forward and more were displaced by Operation Sun Ray in 1995; before this operation, there were 649,000 IDPs (US Committee for Refugees 1996). Many more people were displaced as fighting continued through the following years, and a large number were displaced several times (see Table 9).

Table 9 People displaced in major military operations, 1990-2007

Name of operation	Date of operation	Place of displacement	Number displaced
Sea Breeze	11 June 1990	Batticaloa, Amapari, Jaffna, Mannar, Vavuniya	935,000
Three Forces	17 October 1990	Jaffna	300,000
Valampuri	October 1991	Jaffna islands	70,000
Whirlwind	28 May 1992	Jaffna	20,000
Yarl Devi	September 1993	Kilinochchi, Jaffna	50,000
Leap Forward	9 July 1995	Jaffna	200,000
Handshake	12 September 1995	Jaffna	5,000
Sunray I	15 October 1995	Jaffna	220,000
Sunray II	19 April 1996	Jaffna	250,000
Truth's Victory	August/Sept. 1996	Kilinochchi	200,000
Sun Victory	January 1997	Batticaloa	5,000
Certain Victory	13 May 1998	Vanni	50,000
Sun Power	4 December 1998	Mullaitivu	12,000
Battle Cry	4 March 1999	Vavuniya, Mannar	20,000
Sun Beam	3 September 2000	Vanni	160,000
Anvil	September 2000	Jaffna	65,000
Rod of Fire	25 April 2001	Jaffna	
(Air attacks)	April 2006	Trincomalee	20,000
(Fighting)	August 2006	Trincomalee	50,000
Definite Victory	Nov 2006-Feb 2007	Batticaloa	80,000
Forward Lines	31 August 2007	Mannar/Kilinochchi	120,000

Sources: Sri Lanka Monitor, 1990-2002; Internal Displacement Monitoring Centre; UNOCHA 2008a

Some 800,000 IDPs were receiving state assistance at the time of the ceasefire in 2002, but NGOs estimated the total at one million IDPs (Vije 2004). UNHCR estimated that 917,000 Sri Lankans had sought asylum in 50 countries, including 115,000 in India, of whom 65,000 were in 107 refugee camps in Tamil Nadu (UNHCR 2001). Over 371,000 had returned to their home areas by the end of July 2004, and 11,000 had returned from India (UNHCR 2005).

The entire Eastern Province came under government control after an escalation in the fighting during 2006-2007. This led to the displacement of hundreds of thousands of people, mostly Tamils and Muslims. Fighting intensified in the Northern Province after August 2007 and an increasing number of people were displaced during the first half of 2008 (IDMC 2008a). After April 2006, humanitarian agencies were subjected to a series of restrictions that hampered their ability to access areas where there were IDPs, returnees and other vulnerable groups. Access was largely restricted on security grounds by various armed actors, particularly in LTTE-controlled areas such as the Vanni (Centre for Policy Alternatives 2007), and restrictions continued on goods such as fuel, cement, iron and steel that could strengthen LTTE capabilities (UNOCHA 2008a).

In April 2006, air strikes displaced 20,000 people in Trincomalee. A further 50,000 were displaced as fighting continued into August 2006. Some 80,000 people, many of them IDPs from Trincomalee, were displaced when the army launched an operation to capture Vaharai in Batticaloa. Another 120,000 people were displaced in the military operation to capture LTTE-held areas in Mannar and Kilinochchi. As of September 2008, some 22,000 Tamils had sought refuge in India since 2006, and there were 73,000 Sri Lankan refugees in 117 camps in Tamil Nadu (UNHCR 2008b). Between 2003 and 2007 around 30,300 new Sri Lankan asylum seekers sought refuge elsewhere (UNHCR 2004-2007).

Box 10 A mother sees her son lose his arm

An internally displaced woman in the Vanni describes how an air force attack traumatized her family: "We lived at Vavunikulam until the recent war situation. There was heavy shelling in our village. One day a shell fell closer to our house. We took a decision to leave our village after this incident. We reached Mallavi town at night. We spent about one month there. Mallavi was subjected to heavy shelling. Therefore, we left Mallavi and settled temporarily at Murikandy. We put up a temporary shed there. On September 15, there was heavy shelling around Murikandy and we were forced to flee in the night.

"The next day I went back to Murikandy with my son, a student, and two nephews. While we were removing our temporary shed, a Kfir jet attacked Murikandy. We ran for safety while the Kfir pounded the area. I heard my son loudly crying 'amma, amma'. I ran back and found him severely injured in his right arm. My nephews also suffered leg, arm and head injuries. With the help of others I took them to hospital. In the afternoon, I went back to hospital to see my son. His right arm had been amputated."

Source: Personal communication

The government has applied tremendous pressure on humanitarian agencies working in the region, and many have been forced to leave the region or the island. This is despite the fact that international humanitarian law requires parties to a conflict to assist impartial humanitarian agencies to supply food, medical supplies and other essentials to civilians at risk. The parties must consent to allowing relief operations to take place, and they may not refuse such consent on arbitrary grounds. They can take steps to control the content and delivery of humanitarian aid, such as to ensure that consignments do not include weapons, but deliberately impeding relief supplies is prohibited.

Human Rights Watch therefore called on all sides to instruct civilian officials and military commanders to allow all humanitarian convoys' access to civilians, and to refuse access only when a specific security reason required this. It said refusals for valid security reasons should only be for as long as necessary, and may delay but not block legitimate humanitarian assistance. UNHCR expressed concern that access to IDPs and freedom of movement for civilians, humanitarian agency staff and relief supplies were among the most prominent challenges confronting aid agencies. These resulted not only from security restrictions but also from restrictions on movement into areas under LTTE control and the closure of the A9 road north of Vavuniya, which cut the supply route to Kilinochchi, Mullaitivu and Jaffna (IDMC 2006). Jan Egeland, UN Emergency Relief Coordinator, expressed shock at the lack of access for relief agencies to civilian communities in many conflict areas, and reminded all parties of their international legal obligations to enable unimpeded access to all civilians in need of assistance (Egeland 2006).

In 2008 UN agencies continued to express concern that the A9 road remain closed, leaving Jaffna's civilian population of 632,000 dependent on a limited number of ships and planes for commodities and medicines. Civilian road users are affected by the movements of military convoys, while the high security zones in Jaffna also hinder aid agencies' mobility (UNOCHA 2008b). On 8 September the government, saying it could no longer ensure the safety of aid workers in the LTTE-controlled areas of the Vanni, ordered UN and humanitarian agencies to move staff out to government-controlled territory (AI 2008b).

The security forces have targeted IDPs and many have been killed or disappeared. In 1990, only 45 of over 80 Tamils detained in Trincomalee after army sweeps on refugee camps were accounted for (BRC 1991b). The army rounded up 158 Tamil IDPs sheltering in the Vantharumoolai University refugee camp in Batticaloa on 5 September 1990 and shot them dead (BRC 1990b). On 15 August 1997, the air force bombed refugee settlements in Catholic Church premises at Vavunikulam, killing six Tamils and seriously wounding 17 (BRC 1997e). On 8 November 2006 the army shelled the Vignewara School at Kathiraveli, where some 2000 IDPs had taken refuge, and 62 people died and 47 people were wounded (HRW 2007).

The UN Special Representative on the Internally Displaced observed that IDPs in Sri Lanka are more vulnerable than the rest of the population:"they may be forcibly resettled; more readily subject to round-ups, arbitrary detention and arrests, deprived of their dry rations and more frequently unable to get jobs"(UN Special Representative 1994). It has been noted that they are also vulnerable to disappearances (UN Working Group on Enforced or Involuntary Disappearances 1994).

5.6 Landmines

Extent of unexploded remnants of war including landmines; resulting deaths and injuries; limited demining

Over the years, a large number of civilians have been killed and injured by explosive remnants of war (live munitions that remain after fighting), particularly anti-personnel landmines. Both parties of the conflict have used mines as a defensive weapon, laying them around military

Graph 4 Landmine victims 1996-2006

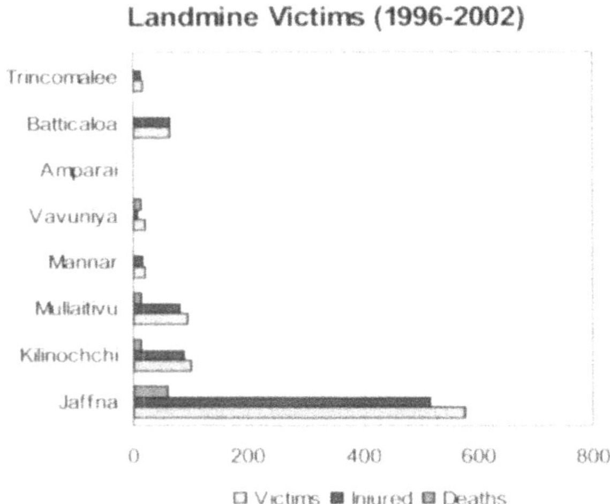

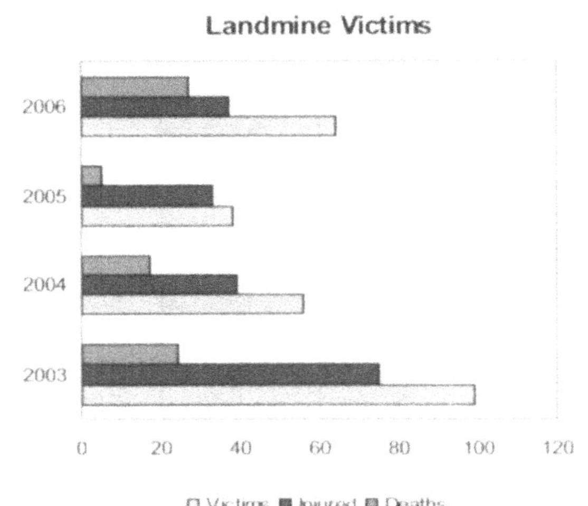

bases and in populated areas (BRC 2003). The extensive mining of agricultural land has contributed to the reduction of a previously vibrant agriculture sector to a survival mode of production (Sarvananthan 2007). Anti-personnel landmines have particularly affected returning IDPs attempting to clear their farmlands and gardens. After the ceasefire agreement in 2002, the estimated number of landmines was one to three million. A 2002 survey of government-controlled areas by the HALO Trust, a UK-based de-mining agency, estimated that the army had laid 900,000 landmines in Jaffna and Kilinochchi, the two worst affected districts (International Campaign to Ban Landmines 2003). The UNDP Information Management System of Mine Action recorded 2577 dangerous areas and minefields in 2003 (ICBL 2007). The Halo Trust said it would take four more years to clear Jaffna of landmines, while the LTTE Humanitarian De-mining Bureau said five years were needed to clear the Vanni region of an estimated 1.5 million landmines over 1570 sq. km. (BRC 2003) - but only 32 sq. km. in the North-East had been cleared by the end of 2006. Ten international and local agencies had cleared 12,421 anti-personnel mines, eleven anti-vehicle mines and 3634 unexploded ordnances (ICBL 2007).

Sixty-four new landmine casualties were recorded in 2006, which excludes victims of indiscriminate claymore mine and roadside bomb attacks. In 2005, there were 38 casulaties and this rose by 65% in the following year, mainly due to the renewal of fighting and a few incidents involving anti-tank mines in Puttalam, Trincomalee and Batticaloa. The number of child casualties accounted for 30% of the total (19 out of 64) compared to an average of 20% in the previous year (US State Department 2007). International agencies estimate that some 900 civilians were killed or maimed by landmines between 1996 and 2002 (Table 10). During the period from 2003 to 2006, 73 civilians were killed by landmines and another 184 were wounded (Table 11).

Table 10 Landmine victims, 1996-2002

District	Victims	Injured	Deaths
Jaffna	577	515	62
Kilinochchi	102	89	13
Mullaitivu	95	82	13
Mannar	21	18	3
Vavuniya	20	8	12
Amparai	5	5	0
Batticaloa	65	65	0
Trincomalee	16	12	4
Total	901	794	107

Sources: Sri Lanka: assessment of needs in the conflict affected areas of the North-East – Asian Development Bank, United Nations and World Bank, 2003

Table 11 Landmine victims, 2002-2006

Year	Victims	Injured	Deaths
2003	99	75	24
2004	56	39	17
2005	38	33	05
2006	64	37	27
Total	257	184	73

Source: International Campaign to Ban Landmines 2001-2006

5.7 Attacks on humanitarian workers
Verbal and physical abuse; lack of accountability; violations of IHL; government restrictions

A large number of international agencies and local NGOs are involved in humanitarian work in Sri Lanka. The Colombo-based Consortium for Relief and Rehabilitation was established in 1984 to coordinate humanitarian work, later became the Consortium of Humanitarian Agencies and was formalized in 1997. A number of international agencies are members and UN agencies have observer status. Some international agencies have been operational in Sri Lanka for more than two decades and include FORUT (Norway), Oxfam (UK), Gesellschaft für Technische Zusammenarbeit (GTZ) (Germany), CARE International (UK), ZOA Refugee Care (Netherlands), and the Danish Red Cross. UN agencies include FAO, UNDP, UNHCR, UNICEF, WFP and WHO. The International Committee of the Red Cross was invited by the Sri Lankan government in 1989. The Sri Lanka Inter-Agency Standing Committee, another mechanism for coordinating humanitarian assistance, involves key UN and non-UN humanitarian partners.

Continuing restrictions and verbal and physical attacks on humanitarian workers have affected their work in many parts of the North-East. The government views humanitarian workers with suspicion. Ministers and officials, particularly those in President Mahinda Rajapakse's administration, have continued to launch verbal attacks against humanitarian workers. Hundreds of human rights defenders, including health workers, have been physically attacked and many have received death threats. In the face of continued threats many have left their homes and localities, and even the country. State agents including the police, army and other law enforcement agencies, for whom successive governments have been directly accountable, continue to perpetrate violations against human rights defenders. For example there have been verbal attacks on humanitarian staff, including UN workers, accusing them of supporting the LTTE (L&ST 2008a).

Attacks on humanitarian workers have continued since the early 1990s. In April 1991, the army fired on a UNHCR vehicle carrying humanitarian aid, alleging that it hid LTTE members (BRC 1991c). Shortly after, Four MSF staff were injured, two seriously, when a military helicopter fired at their clearly marked vehicle on 3 May 1991. In response to international protest, the government appointed a one-man inquiry, which concluded that the team had been on the wrong road during a curfew and that no government personnel were
responsible for "any wrongful act of omission or commission". MSF called the inquiry a whitewash and suspended operations in Sri Lanka until the government could guarantee staff safety (HRW 1992).

After heavy fighting broke out in August 2006, the government enforced new controls on foreign aid workers, ordering all local and foreign NGOs to obtain work permits for expatriate staff by 8 September. A parliamentary select committee was established in 2006 to investigate NGO activities "inimical to the sovereignty and integrity of Sri Lanka" and that "adversely affect Sri Lanka". It has been at the forefront of denouncing NGOs despite the UN Special Representative on Human Rights Defenders' statement that only an independent judicial body should be given authority to review an organization's purpose and determine whether it breaches existing laws (UN Special Representative 2004). In October 2006, on the recommendations of the parliamentary committee, the government decided to withdraw visas issued to members of four international NGOs, alleging that they supported the LTTE.

Between January 2006 and December 2007, 44 humanitarian workers were killed or disappeared, all incidents except one taking place in the North-East. In the other incident, two Sri Lanka Red Cross workers from Batticaloa were abducted at the Fort railway station in Colombo and murdered. Attacks are not always carried out discretely, and in one example, a Norwegian Refugee Council employee was shot dead near an army camp in Vavuniya on 15 May 2006. It is not uncommon for abductions and killings to take place in the vicinity of army checkpoints. On another occassion, 17 workers of the French agency Action Contre la Faim, were murdered in Trincomalee on 5 August 2006. Following the murder of a Red Cross volunteer on 14 December 2007, the EU urged the government to protect humanitarian workers, and to investigate the deaths and bring those responsible to justice (EU 2008).

Male Tamil humanitarian workers aged 21-40 have been the most vulnerable and over a third of all humanitarian workers that have been killed were from Jaffna. The workers killed or disappeared were employees or volunteers of 20 local and international agencies, including the Danish De-mining Group, Halo Trust, Terre des Hommes, United National Office for

Project Services, Sewalanka Foundation, Jesuit Refugee Service and Tamil Rehabilitation Organization (L&S T 2008b; Free Media Movement 2007). Government agencies, security forces or government-aligned paramilitaries are suspected of involvement in many of the killings. The government has failed to carry out proper investigations of any cases, and actively sought to prevent investigation of some cases such as the Action Contre la Faim killings, of which the SLMM said that the security forces were widely and consistently deemed to be responsible.

Three independent UN experts have stated that deliberate targeting of humanitarian workers is a serious violation of the basic principles of international human rights and humanitarian law and the Declaration of Human Rights Defenders (UN Special Representative 2006). The UN has commented that "humanitarian workers are, without question, human rights defenders who help people stay alive during times of conflict" and that "without them, especially in times of conflict, many more civilians would be vulnerable to violations of their civil, cultural, economic, political and social rights such as their right to life, physical integrity, liberty, food, health and adequate housing. In the face of that reality, the responsibility of the Government to extend effective protection to humanitarian workers is heightened" (ibid).

Nevertheless, on 29 August 2006 and without notice, the government froze the bank account of the Tamil Rehabilitation Organization, which works in the North-East. Sri Lankan customs delayed humanitarian aid in Colombo sent to the organization by expatriate Tamils after the tsunami: boat-making equipment, fishing equipment, fire-fighting equipment and snake anti-venom were never released. MSF, having worked in the region for 17 years, withdrew from Jaffna in October 2006 on receiving letters from the government cancelling staff visas and saying the agency was under investigation, with the Sri Lankan media calling the organisation a threat to national security. The Consortium of Humanitarian Agencies received a threat on 20 April 2007 from the Tamil People's Liberation Tigers, a government ally in the Eastern Province.

More recently, UN and humanitarian agencies operating in LTTE areas in the northern Vanni completed withdrawal to army-controlled areas on 16 September 2008, following a Sri Lankan government order (UNOCHA 2008e). The government's NGO secretariat wrote to all registered NGOs saying that no expatriate/employee or any other person employed by an NGO and working in the Vanni would be permitted to travel beyond the Omanthai checkpoint (UNOCHA 2008d). This government call for NGO withdrawal occured despite a statement issued one week earlier expressing concern for the 160,000 IDPs in Mullaitivu and Kilinochchi, including 70,000 who had fled the fighting in the previous two months in the southwestern parts of the Vanni (UN Inter-Agency Standing Committee, 2008). Up till NGO withdrawal, at least 149,000 people were benefitting from the food provided by the WFP (UNOCHA 2008d).

6 The people's health

6.1 Public spending on health and defence

High and increasing defense expenditure; the cost for health and social welfare - declining social expenditure; the defense trap

Militarization over a period of 25 years has affected the entire population of Sri Lanka and had a disastrous impact on the North-East. Sri Lanka is the most militarized country in south Asia (Table 12) - defense expenditure as a percentage of gross domestic product (GDP) is the highest in the region, consistently overtaking social expenditure, and higher than many other nations in conflict (Strategic Foresight 2006). The strategy of 'War for Peace' (i.e. achieving peace through warfare) adopted by the government of President Chandrika Kumaratunge in 1995 resulted in increased defense expenditure and a decrease in social expenditure (Sarvananthan 2002).

Table 12 Military personnel and defense expenditure in South Asia, 2006

Country	Number of military personnel per million population	Average military expenditure as % of GDP	Military Holdings Index*
Bangladesh	1,000	1.5%	198
Nepal	2,700	2.5%	160
India	1,300	2.5%	142
Pakistan	4,000	3.5%	144
Sri Lanka	8,000	4.1%	926

Note * this index measure is based on a country's aggregate number of heavy weapons, such as combat artillery, aircraft, ships, tanks.

Source: Strategic Foresight 2006

Defense expenditure in Sri Lanka has risen dramatically since the 1980s. It increased from LKR16 billion (or US$ 400 million) in 1991 to nearly LKR 70bn (US$770mn) in 2001 - and official figures underestimate the actual expenditure. Secrecy surrounds the whole area of procurement despite repeated demands for information from members of parliament and the media. The Ministry of Defense does not publish annual administrative reports and defence procurements do not follow normal Cabinet tender procedures. The Customs Department does not publish all imports of military hardware and equipment, and the Treasury does not provide details of defence procurements (Sarvananthan 2002). There are also camouflaged military expenditures not included in defense figures. For example, foreign aid is diverted to the war effort - heavy vehicles and equipment from donor-funded infrastructure projects are occasionally used by the army, especially during major military operations. Secondly, the government pays to maintain Tamil militant groups that operate with the security forces; these groups receive concessionary finance through state banks for their business enterprises, and their leaders receive contractual appointments in the public sector. Thirdly, during major battles wounded soldiers are treated in hospitals run by the Defense Ministry, but also in civilian hospitals run by the Health Ministry and the costs incurred by the civilian hospitals are not defrayed by the Defense Ministry (Sarvananthan 2002).

Military expenditure rose from 2% of GDP in 1983 to 6.5% in 1995. It declined to an average of 4.2% during the ceasefire period but remained very high, and rose to 4.6% in 2005 as the war resumed (Table 13). The budgetary allocation for defense in 2006 was LKR 61 bn (USS580mn), a 30% rise on 2005. The allocation for 2007 was more than double the 2006 level - a staggering LKR 139.66 bn (USS1.4bn).

Table 13 Military expenditure in Sri Lanka, 1983-2005

Year	Current GDP	Military expenditure	Government expenditure	Military exp/ GDP	Military exp/ Govt. exp
	(in rupees billions)			% share	
1983	121.6	1.75	N/A	2.0	4.40
1990	321.7	14.60	N/A	5.0	14.60
1995	668.0	43.15	251	6.5	17.19
2000	1,125.0	70.77	453	6.3	15.62
2001	1,245.0	68.29	486	5.5	14.05
2002	1,403.0	64.14	589	4.6	10.89
2003	1,563.0	61.98	661	4.0	9.38
2004	1,798.0	73.45	690	4.1	10.65
2005(est)	1,847.0	84.98	853	4.6	9.96

Source: Strategic Foresight 2006

Sri Lanka has high fiscal deficits, contributing to a serious public debt problem which is undermining the long-term economic health of the country . Despite assistance at concessionary rates, government debt jumped in 2005 from LKR 1864bn to LKR 2127bn, or 107% of GDP (ADB 2005). As defense expenditure increased, social expenditure as a proportion of total public expenditure has been squeezed declining from 13.5% in 1996 to 9.3% in 2001. Expenditure on education decreased from 4.2% to 2.6% and health expenditure from 5% to 3.8%. Poverty alleviation expenditure fell from 3.2% to 2.4% and expenditure on rehabilitation and reconstruction of the North-East from 1.1% to 0.4% (Sarvananthan 2002). The situation is expected to become worse with the resumption of war and rising defense costs, and the government will be unable to allocate sufficient funds to health, education and other social sectors. Table 14 shows defense and social expenditures as a proportion of total public expenditure.

Table 14 Defense and social expenditure

Expenditure	1991	1992	1993	1994	1995	1996	1997	1998	1999	2000	2001
Defence	11.2	12.0	10.9	12.9	14.3	17.7	16.8	16.9	16.4	17.0	14.2
Social	11.2	13.0	9.9	12.8	12.7	13.5	12.6	12.0	12.7	9.8	9.3
1. Education	3.5	5.4	4.3	4.5	3.5	4.2	4.2	4.7	5.0	3.8	2.6
2. Health	2.4	3.1	1.9	2.6	5.2	5.0	4.7	4.0	4.8	3.9	3.8
3. Poverty	5.3	4.5	3.7	5.7	2.0	3.2	3.0	2.5	2.6	2.0	2.4
4. R & R*					2.0	1.1	0.69	0.80	0.27	0.14	0.47

Note * R & R = rehabilitation and reconstruction of the North-East. Poverty and R & R were grouped together 1991-1994.

Source: Economy of the conflict region in Sri Lanka – M Sarvananthan, 2007

The labour-intensive military strategy, mainly intended for controlling territory, has overburdened the economy. Some 80% of the defense budget during 1991-2001 was for recurrent expenditure and only 20% for capital expenditure. The recurrent expenditure for 2001 was LKR 52.5bn (77%) while the capital expenditure was LKR 15.9bn (Table 15) (Sarvananthan 2002).

Table 15 Defence budget, 1991-2001

Year	Recurrent expenditure		Capital expenditure		Total expenditure
	LKR, millions	% of total expenditure	LKR, millions	as % of total expenditure	LKR, millions
1991	12,609	81	3,054	19	15,663
1992	15,627	87	2,369	13	17,996
1993	17,677	85	3,105	15	20,782
1994	21,989	86	3,538	14	25,527
1995	25,815	74	9,156	26	34,971
1996	33,117	72	13,168	28	46,968
1997	35,094	76	10,874	24	45,968
1998	45,314	79	11,832	21	57,146
1999	44,632	82	9,601	18	54,233
2000	57,841	75	19,313	25	77,154
2001	52,537	77	15,977	23	68,514

Source: Economy of the conflict region in Sri Lanka – M Sarvananthan, 2007

Governmnent strategy has seen a huge increase in the number of armed forces. In 2001 there were 300,000 personnel in the security forces, including around 75,000 police, making up about a quarter of the total number of public sector employees. In the same year, there were nearly 1.2 million public sector employees (SLG 2001a). The security forces comprised 2% of the 18.7 million population and 5% of the 6 million-strong labour force. In other words, there were 16 soldiers for every 1000 people. The strategy resulted in a high defense budget trap, as the government cannot cut expenditure significantly even during periods of peace such as the ceasefire (Sarvananthan 2002).

Graph 5 Military Expenditure in Sri Lanka, 1983-2009

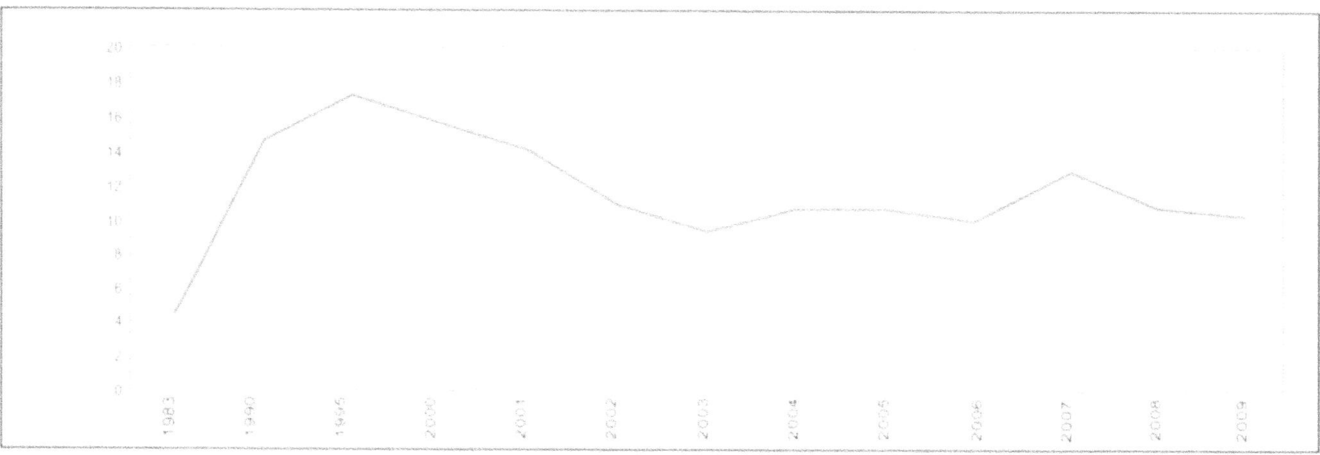

Source: Central Bank of Sri Lanka, Annual Report, 2005, 2006, 2007 & Appropriation Bill, 2009

Alternatively pursuing tax reforms to cover a broader base of households and firms, with the aim to boost tax revenues and cut the budget deficit (and ultimately the public debt burden) has not been successfully pursued. Having large fiscal and external deficits and associated debt burdens leaves the Sri Lankan economy vulnerable in the current global environment. Financing these deficits are particularly difficult given foreign investors risk aversion for a country that already saw credit rating downgrades from both Fitch and Standard & Poor's (to B- and B respectively decsively below investment grade) last year.

Graph 6 Regional Disparities in Military Expenditure in South Asian countries

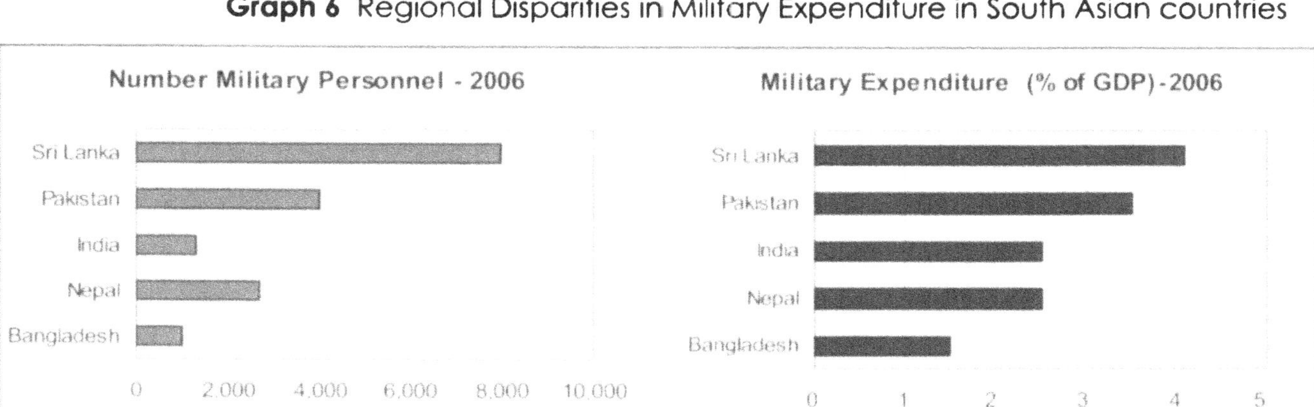

6.2 **Health Information**
Perception and reality: incomplete information

Despite the decline in the share of public expenditure devoted to health, a number of international agencies have praised Sri Lanka's health achievements. According to WHO, for example, Sri Lanka has been known for its achievements in health for several decades, "they are an established fact and have been well documented. Most of the health-related Millennium Development Goals had already been reached on a nationwide basis several years ago" (WHO 2006). A recent British Medical Association publication commends Sri Lanka for achieving "impressive results in health, nutrition and family planning with levels of public health expenditure lower than countries with similar incomes whose health outcomes are considered worse" (2007).

These assessments are based on information provided by the Sri Lankan government - yet its publications on health, including the annual health bulletins of the Department of Health Services, often contain inaccurate or misleading information on health in the North-East (see Box 10 and Appendix 2 for some examples). The Sri Lankan state's 106-page report to the UN Committee on Economic Social and Cultural Rights (1997) was silent on the malnutrition in the North-East districts. This was noted by Foodfirst Information and Action Network

---

Box 11 Regional Disparities

While Sri Lanka's key indicators in areas such as life expectancy, infant and maternal mortality, school enrolment and literacy appear to be acceptable, national figures do disguise disparities between regions. Most significantly, national figures do not include conflict-affected districts in the North-East, which represent 13 percent of the population and include some of the most deprived regions in the country. Deprived districts in the southern central part of the country also receive little attention despite some of the lowest human development indicator values.

With the country's Gross National Income (GNI) exceeding the threshold of USD 826 per capita, Sri Lanka is considered a lower middle-income country. However, these figures obscure significant disparities between geographical regions. A total of 22.7 per cent of the population is considered to be living below the official poverty line.

And together with poverty, malnutrition is of key concern in Sri Lanka, both issues being interlinked. On average, an estimated 29.4 per cent of children are reported to be underweight , however, in selected deprived districts average estimates are 37.4 per cent . The net primary school enrolment rate is 96.4 per cent , and shows no significant gender related difference, but yet there are vast disparities with regards to the quality of education. Only 24 per cent of children in the conflict affected North-East have achieved mastery level in their first language, the highest percentage being registered with just above 50 per cent in the Western Province that hosts the capital.

'Appendix 2: When official statistics fall silent' further details the gaps in data for the North-East region.

Source: UNICEF (2008b)

International in its report to the 17th session of the committee in 1997, and also observes that government surveys on nutrition excluded the eight districts of the North-East (BRC 1997g). WHO recognises that the 2000 Annual Health Bulletin provides no data on the North-East, excepting Amparai district, and noted that the epidemiological and family planning information provided in four tables "can be said to be grossly under-reported or inaccurate". Thus WHO has advised caution in interpreting the data (WHO 2002). The Sri Lankan human rights agency, the Law and Society Trust, has repeatedly challenged the poor quality of government health information (see Box 12).

After 1981, national census, socioeconomic and poverty surveys and demographic health surveys by government institutions exclude either the whole of or parts of the North-East. The Director General of Health Services, introducing the 1994 Annual Health Bulletin, says that a good management information system is a prerequisite for the managerial process for health development at national and sub-national levels. However, nine statistical tables in the bulletin exclude the Northern and Eastern provinces. The 2002 bulletin makes claim that data had been revised and brought up to date to reflect as far as possible the situation in 2002 - but neglects to mention that the northern and eastern districts are not represented by the statistical data. The exclusion of the North-East skews health statistics throughout the 1990s, a trend that has continued in the new millennium.

Box 12 Criticisms of government health information

The Sri Lankan human rights agency, the Law and Society Trust, has repeatedly challenged the quality of government health information, as follows:

1993 - "In recent times, the reliability of health statistics has been in question… many aspects of the health situation do not get recorded since all health problems do not necessarily get directed to formal health institutions… conditions prevailing as a result of the conflict would affect the health standards achieved, but it is not clear how far these situations are covered by present surveys."

1995 - "Verifiable data from the North-East is not available to make a proper analysis of the people's right to access health care in these areas."

1998 - "Comprehensive data on health and health services in the North-East is not available…"

1999 - "Since Government officials are not willing to travel to these areas, it is unable to assess and identify the needs of people living in these areas."

2000 - "Sri Lanka's health indicators appear to be among the best in South Asia. However, the accuracy of these official health status indicators is doubtful. For example 24% of maternal deaths (in the Western Province) are not recorded… the rate of under-reporting deaths in different parts of the country ranged from 27.5% to 53.7%. The under-reporting of infant deaths was very high and ranged from 64% to 90.9%."

Source: Law and Society Trust 1994, 1996, 1999, 2000, 2001

The 2006-2007 demographic and health survey omits five districts in the Northern Province (UNOCHA 2008f), while the 2008 report on poverty by the Department of Census and Statistics and the Ministry of Finance and Planning excludes the five northern districts and Trincomalee in the east (SLG 2008b).

It is acknowledged that data collection in conflict zones is difficult. But transparency is expected of the government and genuine efforts must be made to compile data and/or to be clear about what is not included. A number of international agencies were operating in these areas during the phases of data collection and their assistance could have been sought. There should be no undue pressure on health institutions and health professionals in conflict zones which might prevent the release of information. The government should also refrain from using data collected in a part of the country only to compile national health statistics for international information purposes.

6.3 Population health

Increased health risks: mortality and morbidity, malnutrition, inequalities; lack of resources and effect on health; snakebite; mental health – the effects of conflict

In 2002, the health status of the population of the North-East was continuing to deteriorate, with the following particular areas of risk (WHO 2002):

- increase in the virulent form of malaria (Plasmodium falciparum) due to interruption of the vector control programme,
- increase in the incidence of acute respiratory infections and diarrhoeal diseases, owing to inadequate shelter; damage or disruption to water and sanitation systems; and insanitary and crowded conditions in IDP camps
- worsening of maternal and child health, especially nutritional status, owing to food shortages; deterioration of public health services; non-functioning of maternal and child health programmes; and the psychological impact of conflict,
- psychological trauma associated with conflict and violence and the associated displacement, deaths of family and friends, disintegration of families and communities, and loss of property,
- disability due to war-related injuries and
- unreliability of data on leading causes of hospitalization and deaths.

This situation marginally improved during the ceasefire, but conditions are again deteriorating rapidly as result of the resumption of fighting, continuing restrictions, new blockades and inadequate tsunami recovery operations.

Infant and child mortality

Childhood mortality is a key indicator of socioeconomic level and quality of life. The infant mortality rate (the number of infants dying aged under one year, expressed as the number of deaths per 1000 live births) in the North-East is much higher than the island-wide average (World Bank 2004). In Jaffna district the rate was eleven in 1985 but had increased to more than 22 by 2000; the average in the North-East was nearly fifteen in 2000 and much higher in some districts (Table 16). In contrast, the national figure fell from 24 in 1985, to fifteen in 1998, and to eleven in 2003.

Table 16 Infant mortality in North-East Sri Lanka, 2000

Region		Infant deaths per 1000 live births
North-East		14.7
North	Jaffna	22.3
	Kilinochchi	27.8
	Mannar	22.3
	Mullaitivu	20.3
	Vavuniya	8.8
East	Amparai	10.3
	Batticaloa	15.8
	Trincomalee	4.6

Source: WHO 2002

Maternal mortality

Socioeconomic factors such as poverty, illiteracy, malnutrition and the low social status of women are important underlying causes of maternal death (Hafez 1998), compounded by obstetric complications and diseases developed during pregnancy. All these factors are exacerbated during violent conflict. Maternal deaths have been falling in the rest of the country, but increasing in the North-East. The maternal mortality ratio for both Jaffna and Sri Lanka was 51 per 100,000 live births in 1980, but by 1996 it was 80 and 23 respectively (WHO 2002). It rose to an average 81 in the North-East by 2000, reaching 158 in Kilinochchi (see Table 17), whereas in Sri Lanka as a whole it fell to 14 in 2002.

Table 17 Maternal mortality in North-East Sri Lanka, 2000

Region		Maternal deaths per 100,000 live births
North-East		81
North	Jaffna	62
	Kilinochchi	158
	Mannar	97
	Mullaitivu	123
	Vavuniya	76
East	Amparai	24
	Batticaloa	117
	Trincomalee	57

Source: WHO 2002

Graph 7 Maternal mortality & infant mortality

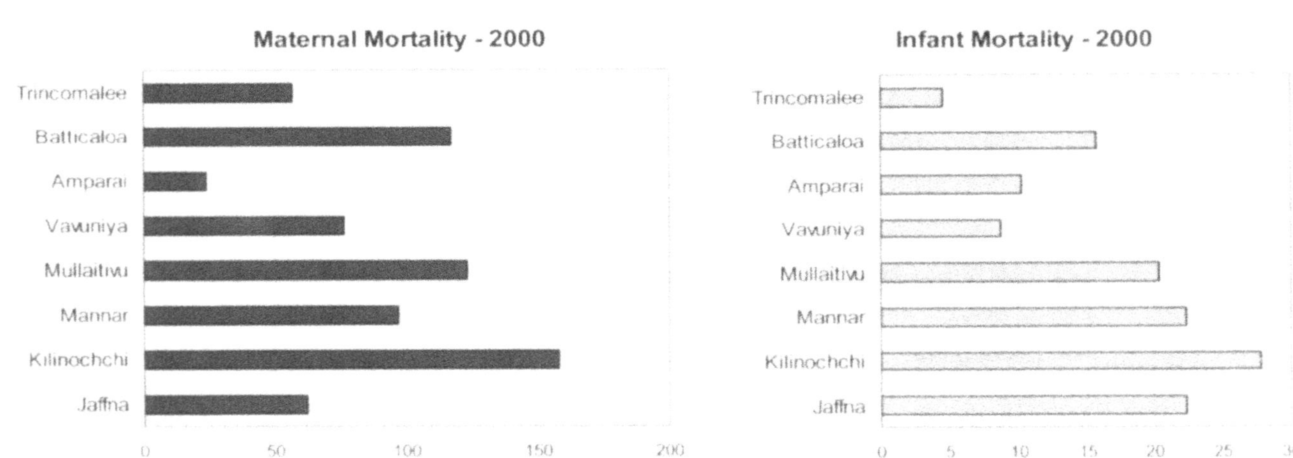

Nutrition

Malnutrition places children at increased risk of morbidity, mortality and impaired mental development. Severe acute malnutrition among under-fives in parts of conflict-affected Batticaloa and Jaffna districts is 6-7% while the national average is 2.5% (SLG 2000, UNICEF 2008).

Nationally, close to 17% of newborn babies in 2001 were underweight, but in the North-East the figure was nearly 26%, and largely associated with maternal undernutrition. In Vavuniya almost 30% were underweight, and 31% in Trincomalee. In the whole of Sri Lanka, 29% of children under five were underweight (low weight for age) in 2001, but in the North-East the figure was 46%. Specifically, in Batticaloa 53% of children under five were underweight, in

Graph 8 Malnutrition in children, Trincomalee district, 1999

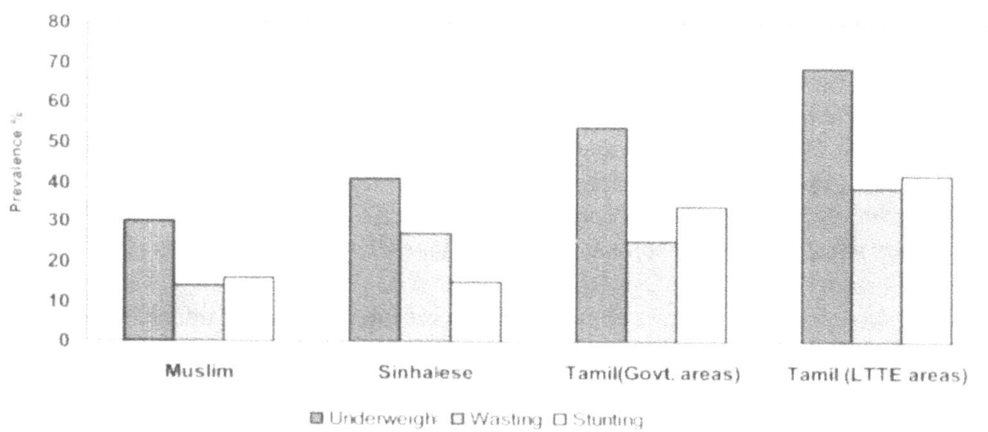

Trincomalee nearly 45%, in Jaffna 43% and in Vavuniya almost 51%.
Source: Integrated Food Security Programme 2000

The prevalence of underweight, wasting (acute malnutrition) and stunting (chronic malnutrition) among children under five in Sri Lanka were 31%, 13% and 16% respectively in 1995-6. It is highly likely the rates were worse in the North-East, caused by food shortages, unclean water, poor hygiene and difficulties in accessing health services. This is indicated by the results of a survery carried out in Trincomalee by the Integrated Food Security Programme in 1999. The survey reported underweight, wasting and stunting rates of 51%, 27% and 28% respectively, and very high malnutrition among women and children, in a sample of 515 households which included 702 children. The Programme found that, of the children whose birth weight was recorded, 19% weighed less than 2500 grams, and observed they would have greater difficulty in gaining the appropriate weight in their early years. The highest prevalence of low birth weight (38%) was among Tamil children in LTTE-controlled areas, where one in four children had a low birth weight (IFSP 2000). The survey also found that Tamil children in LTTE-controlled areas had more underweight, wasting and stunting problems than those in other sectors of the population (Table 18).

Table 18 Malnutrition in children, Trincomalee district, 1999*

	Muslim	Sinhalese	Tamil (govt. areas)	Tamil (LTTE areas)
Underweight	30	41	54	69
Wasting	14	27	25	39
Stunting	16	15	34	42

Note * Prevalence %
Source: Integrated Food Security Programme 2000

Malnutrition continues to affect the region. The official 2006-7 demographic and health survey (SLG 2008a) excludes the Northern Province, where malnutrition levels are among the highest in the country. Stunting, the outcome of a failure to receive adequate nutrition over an extended period, is also affected by recurrent or chronic illness. According to the survey, 18% of Sri Lankan children are stunted and 4% are severely stunted. In Batticaloa 24% of children are stunted and 8% severely stunted, and in Trincomalee the figures are 31% and 11% respectively.

Children whose weight for height is below -2 SD (see Table 19) are considered wasted (or thin). Wasting represents the failure to receive adequate nutrition in the period immediately before the survey and typically results from recent illness, especially diarrhoea, or a rapid deterioration in food supplies. 15% of Sri Lankan children are wasted, 3% are severely wasted. Excluding the Northern Province, wasting is highest in Trincomalee, where 28% are wasted and 10% are severely wasted.

Children whose weight-for-age is below -2 SD (see Table 19) are considered underweight, a measure reflecting the effects of both acute and chronic malnutrition. 22% of Sri Lankan children are underweight, 4% severely underweight (SLG 2008a). Excluding the Northern Province, Batticaloa and Trincomalee have the highest percentage of underweight children in Sri Lanka (SLG 2008a).

Table 19 Nutritional status of children, 2006-7 survey*

District	Height for age (stunting)		Weight for height (wasting)		Weight for age (underweight)	
	Below -3 SD	Below -2 SD	Below -3 SD	Below -2 SD	Below -3 SD	Below -2 SD
Amparai	2.7	14.1	4.7	19.3	2.1	22.0
Batticaloa	7.7	24.4	6.7	19.4	5.5	27.5
Trincomalee	11.3	30.5	10.2	28.1	6.4	27.8
Sri Lanka	4.2	17.9	3.0	15.0	3.8	21.6

Note: * Percentage prevalence
Source: Sri Lanka Government 2008a, Table 12

Nutritional status has deteriorated sharply in the North-East. Jaffna had the lowest malnutrition levels according to a 1975-1976 national survey (SLG 1976). By 1992, wasting was 19%, and by 2000 wasting among children of 6-18 months was 31% (WHO 2002). Studies showed 26% of children were wasted, 27% stunted and 50% underweight in Trincomalee in 1999; over 19% of displaced children were wasted in Vavuniya in 2000 (IFSP 1999); and 22% wasted and 36% stunted in IDP camps in Jaffna in 2001 (WFP 2001). Dr Ines Reinhard, an IFSP doctor working in Trincomalee, told a meeting on 22 June 2001 in Trincomalee that 80% of the population of the North-East lived under the poverty line, and malnutrition was significantly higher than the national average. Half of all women were malnourished and 30% of children suffered from Vitamin A deficiency in some areas in Trincomalee. In 2008, UNICEF said 14% of children under five in Sri Lanka showed signs of wasting and stunting, while 29% were underweight for age. It is known that districts affected by conflict have higher rates (UNOCHA 2008c).

Box 13 No shelter from the monsoon

Thousands of displaced people are in desperate need of shelter, food and sanitation, Amnesty International reported in 2008. As the North-East monsoon season approached, only 2100 temporary shelters had been provided for 4000 families, leaving at least 20,000 families without protection from the elements. Over 300,000 people faced the next few months crowded together in temporary shelters, surrounded by mud, with no promise of regular access to food or adequate sanitation. The situation in the Vanni in northern Sri Lanka was rapidly becoming critical.

The Sri Lankan government said it was distributing aid to displaced families. Amnesty International, however, said the government lacked the capacity to uphold international standards on human rights and to ensure support was provided to protect the lives of thousands of people. It called on the government to end its policy of blocking humanitarian aid.

Source: Amnesty International 2008c

Diseases and deaths

Throughout the 1990s hospitals in the North-East struggled to function due to insufficient medicines and medical equipment. Malnutrition and a lack of immunization increased the risk of disease. Malaria, diarrhoea and septicaemia were major causes of death in hospitals. The Vanni area was particularly affected. From April to June 1991, 540 people died in Jaffna hospital (BRC 1992). According to the Jaffna Regional Health Director 270 newborn babies died in the Jaffna peninsula in November 1994 due to a lack of medical facilities, three children died of septicaemia in December in Jaffna hospital, and eight others of dengue fever (BRC 1994). In June 1996, the Jaffna Hospital Director called for urgent upgrading of health facilities in the peninsula to prevent diseases such as malaria, typhoid and diarrhoea (BRC 1996d).

The lack of medicines and medical equipment caused the death of 22 people in Vanni's Mallavi hospital within a week in August 1996. These people had been sent to Mallavi hospital after Kilinochchi hospital was closed when the Sri Lankan army launched Operation Sathjaya (BRC 1996d). MSF struggled to treat around 1,000 outpatients a day in an improvised clinic in Akkarayankulam. Over 40% of the patients suffered from increasing levels of diarrhoea and malaria (BRC 1996e). MSF expressed concern in June 1997 that Akkarayankulam and Mallavi hospitals did not receive the medicines requested from the government and children were deprived of immunization. 61 people died in Akkarayankulam hospital in May and June (BRC 1997c). Six IDP children died in an outbreak of diarrhoea in Mannar District in July 1997 which also affected 160 others (BRC 1997e).

Over the 1990s, the health situation in the North-East became progressively critical, with increasing acute health problems and severe malnutrition (Christian Aid 1998). During 1997 and 1998, 53% of the country's 430,240 malaria patients were from Mullaitivu, Kilinochchi and Jaffna districts, where 80% of the 177 deaths due to malaria occurred (BRC 2000a). In Mullaitivu district 339,000 out of 727,000 hospital patients were treated for malaria; many had suffered repeated infections leading to debility, brain haemorrhage and outbreaks of tuberculosis. Increases in rates of septicaemia, typhoid and diarrhea were reported. Between December 1998 and January 1999, 33 people died of malaria and diarrhea in Puthukudyiruppu (BRC 1998f). When the transfer of patients from the Vanni to Vavuniya hospital was blocked in June 1999, following the launch of Operation Rana Gosh IV, eight people died in the Vanni without proper medical care (BRC 1999g).

During November 1999, the mortality rate among the 710 patients admitted to Mallavi hospital was 4%, and the rate for children under twelve years was 6.5%. Some 150 patients were admitted to the surgical ward, but only 46 major operations were carried out as medical supplies ran out. Eight civilians died in the same month from shell blast injuries, including two following surgery; seven children under the age of twelve also died in the hospital (BRC 1999c). In 1999, Mallavi hospital treated 158,300 people, many for malaria, septicaemia and diarrhea, and 142 people died in the hospital. In the same year 216,000 people were treated in Kilinochchi hospital, including 31,617 for malaria, and there were186 deaths including of 17 children (BRC 2000b). In June 2000, Kilinochchi hospital treated 15,970 people for malaria, diarrhea and other diseases and ten people died as a result of lack of medicines (BRC 2000c).

Death and disease continue to ravage the population, especially IDPs who lack the basics needed to protect their health including food, shelter and sanitation (see example in Box 13).

Malaria

Malaria remained a major problem in the North-East in 2002, with 50-62% of reported malaria cases in the whole island occurring in the region (WHO 2002). In the same year 30 deaths due to malaria were reported nationally, of which 25 deaths were in the North-East (SLG 2002b). 76 deaths from malaria were reported to the Sri Lanka Anti-Malarial Campaign in 2000, of which 70 (92%) occurred in the North-East (SLG 2000). According to the Department of Health Services, the increased morbidity and mortality from malaria in these areas was mainly due to practical conflict-related difficulties in case detection, treatment and control (SLG 2000), but government restrictions on chemicals used in prevention and medicines for treatment were also a factor. Chlorine and anti-malarial chemicals such as malathion were banned in the northern areas in the early 1990s, and such restrictions on public health items has resulted in an increase in cases of malaria (Save the Children 1998).

Snakebites

Snakebites are a major cause of morbidity and mortality in Sri Lanka, particularly in rural and agricultural areas. Snakebite venom can damage the nervous system, kidneys, blood vessels and the heart, cause weakness of the muscles and affect the body's mechanism for blood clotting (Seneviratne 2002). The conflict and its consequences have created severe difficulties for the treatment of snakebite victims. Many victims have died as they could not be treated because of military restrictions on movement, checkpoints or curfews. Some of those brought to health centres and hospitals have died as a result of lack of anti-venom (see Box 14).

A study of 14,500 people admitted to Kilinochchi Hospital between January and November 2005 revealed that 303 had been bitten; of these 145 (48%) demonstrated local pain and swelling, 134 (44%) developed a prolonged clotting time and 46 (15%) developed ptosis (abnormal drooping of the upper eyelid), indicating weakness of the nervous system. Respiratory failure occurred in five victims, who were intubated, hand-ventilated and transferred to Jaffna (Whitehall et al 2007).

Box 14 Snakebite deaths in a village

"I came across many snakebite deaths when I worked seven years in the Vavuniya District Development Office, which served 137 villages. Villages such as Kovil Kunchukulam, lying north-west of Omanthai, were virtually cut off due to military restrictions and violence. The health centre in Kovil Kunchukulam had no nurses and lacked basic medical facilities. I visited the village in late December 2003. In the first week of December, a boy aged 13 suffered snakebite while sleeping at his home. The parents rushed him to the health centre. But he could not be saved because the centre had no proper medicines. Ten days later a man was bitten by a snake while going to draw water from the well. He was also taken to the health centre, but died later. Another man was stung at home during the last week of December. The villagers had lost faith in the health centre and took him to the village medicine man. But the medicine man could not save him either."

Source: Personal communication from an employee of the Vavuniya District Development Office

---

Mental health

Violent conflict creates huge psychological problems. Deaths, injuries, disappearances, torture and threats to life and property have had a major impact on the mental health of victims and their families and friends in North-East Sri Lanka. The deafening sound of multi-barrel rocket launchers in continuous use by security forces is having an adverse effect on vulnerable sections of the population. Psychological disturbances, particularly depressive symptoms, are more common in displaced families than in those living in their own homes. Repeated displacement and disruption of livelihoods have made people dependent on handouts. Women are suffering from somatization (chronic and persistent complaints of varied physical symptoms that have no identifiable physical origin), depression following loss of loved ones, property or dignity, anxiety and post-traumatic stress disorder (Somasundaram 2003). Those obliged to shoulder additional responsibilities without adequate material and psychological support are particularly vulnerable. Children have been traumatized by frequent experiences of deaths, injuries, shelling, helicopter strafing, round-ups, cordon and search operations, mass arrests, detention, shootings, grenade explosions and landmines. They have also been affected by recruitment to participate in the war (Somasundaram 2002).

A 2001 study of children in the Eastern Province found that 41% had personally experienced conflict-related violence (such as having their home attacked or shelled, being shot at, beaten, or arrested). Over half had direct family members killed violently, including disappearances of family members following abduction or detention. Nearly all had personal experience of or had witnessed actual or threatened death, serious injury, and other threats to the integrity of self or others and 92% of these events were directly conflict-related. Severe (20%) and moderate (39%) levels of post-traumatic psychological distress were found and similar levels of depression and unresolved grief reactions were observed. Many children disclosed traumatic experiences previously held as secrets from family members and other adults (Chase and Bush 2001).

A mental health needs assessment in 1999-2000 in IDP camps in Vavuniya found a high number of attempted suicides, alcohol abuse, domestic violence, grief, suspicion and a sense of 'learnt helplessness'; a breakdown in social support networks; appalling living conditions and lack of services; and a complete lack of psychological support services. Of the group surveyed, 97% had lost their homes and property, 87% had constant feelings of insecurity, 63% had experienced suicidal thoughts and 66% had bad memories, for example of displacement, death of a family member, and witnessing people being burnt alive in their homes. The suicide rate in the camps (103 per 10,000) was almost three times higher than in the community (37 per 10,000) (MSF 2002).

A WHO mental health needs assessment in North-East Sri Lanka in 2003 concluded that, although the Ministry of Health had given mental health top priority in the region, no concrete steps had been taken. Twenty years of conflict had severely impaired or destroyed service development for people with severe mental illness, resulting in under-provision and fragmentation of services. The region had no appropriate psychosocial rehabilitation facilities for people who need intermediate (up to six months) inpatient care following acute treatment, or for people with chronic schizophrenia. They were at risk of neglect or of becoming long-stay residents in the Colombo-based psychiatric hospitals, where treatment was inadequate and patients tended to deteriorate in the absence of psychosocial rehabilitation or social support (WHO 2003). WHO made the following recommendations, but the mental health care system deteriorated further as the government did not take adequate steps to implement them:

- Give priority to the development of normal community-based mental health services to address severe mental illness and common mental disorders and problems, including trauma-related.
- Increase efforts to attract and retain mental health professionals.
- Establish functioning acute inpatient psychiatry units in general hospitals in each district. This activity includes building or repairing/refurbishing units in seven districts, hiring ward nurses and auxiliary staff where needed, and installing a telephone hotline in each unit.
- Organize monthly follow-up outpatient clinics for severely mentally ill people.
- Organize care in the community for people with common mental disorders and heavy alcohol and drug use (including trauma-related problems). This involves training and supervision of primary health care staff, teachers, village leaders and traditional healers.

Torture survivors develop many physical and psychiatric symptoms, including post-traumatic stress disorder and co-morbidities such as somatization, anxiety and depression, personality destruction, deep suspicion and mistrust of the world, severe social withdrawal, impaired interpersonal relationships and poor social skills. Severe phobia, avoidance of any stimulus that evokes re-experiencing the torture, sleep disturbances with nightmares and night terrors, impaired memory and concentration are frequent symptoms (Somasundaram 2008).

Facilities for the rehabilitation of torture victims are lacking. The UN Special Rapporteur on Torture, visiting in 2007, urged the government to establish such centres (UN Special Rapporteur 2008). Medical specialists and victims' organizations met in Jaffna in 2008 nd urged the authorities and international agencies to provide adequate psychological treatment.

7 Health services

7.1 The health system
Health structures; shortages of supplies and personnel

The Provincial Councils Act (1989) devolved responsibility for health and entrusted the Provincial Ministry of Health Services with the provision of health services, bar teaching hospitals. However there has been no provincial government since 1990 in the North-East, and the powers and functions of such a council were exercised by the President through central government administrative bodies. Decisions are taken in Colombo without consultation on local needs and often in furtherance of political considerations. A provincial council was elected on 10 May 2008 for the Eastern Province, but the Northern Province still has no provincial government.

By 2002 the shortages of health personnel, basic facilities and support systems were impeding health care delivery in the North-East especially in remote and rural areas (WHO 2002). In 2008, Jaffna residents could not obtain certain health care services on the peninsula, and the ICRC airlifted patients between Jaffna and Colombo twice a week. In March 2008 alone, 54 patients requiring specialized surgery, medical tests or treatment, accompanied by 35 carers and 10 medical staff from the Jaffna Teaching Hospital, were transported to Colombo on ICRC-chartered flights (ICRC 2008). The Jaffna Teaching Hospital lies within army-controlled areas. No such service is available for people in LTTE-controlled areas.

Preventive care is provided by health teams headed by the medical officer of health or divisional director of health services for a population of 60-100,000, public health nurses and inspectors for a population of 8-10,000, and family health workers (i.e. midwives) for a population of 3000. Staff shortages and a lack of basic facilities and support undermine preventive care.

The LTTE, in territory under its control, developed the Tamil Eelam Health Service for the civilian population and internally displaced people in addition to its military medical section. This complemented the state health service, running primary care services and limited secondary care services. It introduced mobile clinics to access remote villages, laying special emphasis on preventive medicine. Its medical training programme produced 'medics' who began as first-aid providers and developed into specialists in war trauma, providing comprehensive trauma clinics (Whitehall 2007).

7.2 Health facilities
Infrastructural damage; armed forces involvement; lack of access

After the February 2002 ceasefire it was found that 56 of the 405 health institutions in the North-East had been destroyed and 51 were not functioning, as reported by international agencies such as WHO but not in the 2002 Annual Health Bulletin. In Batticaloa seven out of 38 health institutions had been destroyed and five were not functioning; in Mannar seven out of 30 had been destroyed and twelve were not functioning. Kilinochchi, Mullaitivu and Jaffna were the worst affected. In Kilinochchi, seven out of 18 institutions had been destroyed and four were not functioning; in Mullaitivu, 21 out of 28 had been destroyed and two were not functioning; in Jaffna, nine out of 77 had been destroyed and 21 were not functioning. In Mullaitivu, all thirteen Gramodhya health centres had been destroyed, and in Jaffna thirteen of the 84 Gramodhaya health centres had been destroyed. In Batticaloa five of the fifteen central dispensaries and in Mannar five of the central dispensaries had been destroyed. In Mullaitivu, two of three maternity homes and in Kilinochchi two of four maternity homes had been destroyed. One district hospital in each of Mullaitivu, Mannar, Kilinochchi and Jaffna districts had been destroyed.

Box 15 Nothing obscured the suffering

Dr John Whitehall, a leading paediatrician from Australia, recently spent five months in Sri Lanka on a humanitarian mission. He describes his impressions:

"Driving north from Colombo to Jaffna, I was struck by the poverty on the Tamil side of the armed border, the lack of facilities in the Hospital in Kilinochchi (the administrative centre of the 'Tamil' land) and the dilapidation of the tertiary hospital in Jaffna."

"Only the crowds in the corridors and the patients on the floors obscured the filth on the walls and passageways. Nothing obscured the suffering of apparently half-dead people being carried on bare metal stretchers at perilous angles up and down the stairs, buffeted in the surge. I was struck by the whites of their fingers as they clung to the metal. Nothing prevented the recycling of dengue through unscreened windows from sewage that pooled from broken pipes alongside the wards. One piddling tap leaned vainly against cross-infection in the crowded children's barn. Why was this hospital so different to the many I had visited in the Sinhalese areas? I later learned of economic sanctions and under-funding by Colombo."

Source: Whitehall 2007

Security forces have been directly responsible for the destruction of many health institutions. In Operation Whirlwind in Jaffna in 1992, the Tellippalai Co-operative Hospital, the Mallakam Rural Development Society Building (where clinics of the Tellipalai Government Hospital were held), the Vigneswara Dispensary and Surgery in Chunnakam and the American Mission Hospital were damaged in bombing and shelling (Vije 1993). In 107 days of continued aerial bombardment in Jaffna city alone, buildings, equipment and medicines belonging to the health sector, estimated at LKR 17 million, were destroyed (Engineering Consultancy Bureau, Jaffna 1991). The School Health Officer's office, the Central Dispensary and Maternity Home and Jaffna General Hospital sustained damage. Myliddy TB Hospital, Pannai Chest Hospital and Tellippalai Cancer Hospital were destroyed (Vije 1993). The UK medical agency Merlin reported that Jaffna Hospital and 5% of all buildings in the town had been severely damaged (BRC 1996b). The air force attacked houses near Kilinochchi General Hospital at Anandapuram on 2 November 2006, killing five civilians and forcing 500 patients to flee.

Table 20 Numbers of health personnel, 2001-2002

North-Eastern District*	Staff needed	In post	Vacancies
Amparai	2,315	1634	670
Batticaloa	1,499	1289	212
Trincomalee	1,331	1142	178
Vavuniya	712	499	191
Mannar	800	298	502
Kilinochchi	551	-	263
Mullaitivu	382	238	140
Jaffna	2,836	1550	1,003
Total	**10,426**	**6650**	**3,251**

* 31 December 2001
Sources: WHO 2002, Sri Lanka Government 2002

Table 21 Health personnel shortages in the North-East, 2001

Category	Number needed	Number in post	Vacancies
Medical officer of health	402	311	91
Dental surgeon (specialist)	7	0	7
Assistant medical officer	261	148	113
Pharmacist	133	76	57
Public health inspector	323	261	62
Nursing officer A & B	1070	545	525
Public health nursing sister	63	5	58
School dental therapist	37	25	12
Supervising public health midwife	70	4	66
Public health midwife	1155	647	508
Medical laboratory technologist	59	37	22
Malaria supervisor	12	0	12

Source: WHO 2002

In 2002, WHO have reported that some medical institutions were closed because of shortages of staff and medicines or security reasons (because they lie within a security zone or are occupied partly or fully by security forces), while hospitals were dilapidated and deteriorating for want of maintenance. Most buildings were 50-80 years old and lacked adequate water supplies, sewerage systems, basic equipment and supplies (WHO 2002). A recent first-hand account by an Australian paediatrician highlights the appalling conditions (Box 15).

Military camps and road blocks have been established near hospitals, restricting access for patients, particularly at night (Sivarajah 2001). Myliddy TB Hospital and the cancer hospital at Varuthalaivilan in Jaffna have been shut down. High security zones have also caused hospitals to be shifted to places where facilities are inadequate, for instance some hospital departments have been relocated to schools, and are then unable to function. The main hospital in Tellipalai, Jaffna was shifted to the co-operative hospital building in the same area in 1991 because of the creation of a zone. The hospital administrative officer describes the situation in 2002: "with this small building, we can't function properly. Earlier, our hospital had 290 beds, a district medical officer, 14 medical officers, two dental surgeons and 62 nurses. Now we have only 102 beds. The district medical officer is the only medical officer. There are two less qualified registered medical officers, two retired registered medical officers and 13 nurses" (Aravinthan 2003).

7.3 Human resources for health

Vacancies; inappropriate recruiting; inequalities in human resource ratios

International agencies assessing war damage noted in 2003 that more than 3000 vacant posts in the North-East, mainly in skilled and professional categories including medical officers, basic specialists and paramedical workers, had not been filled (ADB et al 2003). Doctors and other health workers were unwilling to work there because of fear, insecurity, and lack of accommodation and non-payment of incentives (WHO 2002). Table 20 indicates the health personnel needed in North-Eastern districts and unfilled vacancies at the beginning of 2002, whilst Table 21 shows the number of staff needed in the same period, by occupation.

The shortage of paramedics in the region is also due to lack of recruitment of Tamil speaking persons and lack of training in the Tamil language. Training courses for medical laboratory technologists, physiotherapists and school dental therapists are held in Colombo and mostly conducted in the Sinhala language. Students from the North-East who only speak Tamil often drop out (Sivarajah 2001), and many are too afraid to train in Colombo as some students from the region have been arrested and tortured in Colombo.

There are two nursing education centres in the North-East, in Jaffna and Batticaloa, but Tamils are discriminated against by the Ministry of Health, which controls selection. The Ministry selected 75 students in 1998 for training as family health workers in the Tamil language medium in Jaffna, but only four turned up - 45 did not know Tamil, while 26 were from other districts and were unwilling to train in Jaffna (WHO 2002). WHO also says the full capacity of facilities for training nurses and family health workers is not utilized. Furthermore, applications and invitations for training are often delayed, sometimes for many months, because of the Colombo-based centralization of student selection, bureaucratic delays in processing applications, and postal difficulties in the North-East, and many applicants move on to other employment. The two centres have the capacity to train 100 nurses and 100 family health workers (Sivarajah 2001), but the mean annual output in 1991-2002 was only 38 nurses and 13 family health workers (see Table 22).

In 2002, only 30 (4%) of Sri Lanka's 669 specialist doctors in curative services worked in the North-East of the country. Kilinochchi and Mannar had none, Vavuniya had one general surgeon and one obstetrician, Amparai had one obstetrician and one paediatrician. There were no cardiologists, dermatologists, chest physicians, paediatric surgeons, orthopaedic surgeons, plastic surgeons, genito-urinary surgeons, neurosurgeons, thoracic surgeons, pathologists, microbiologists and bacteriologists, radiotherapists, oncologists or radiologists.

The official 2002 Annual Health Bulletin said the total number of medical officers rose from 6994 in 1999 to 9549 in 2002, thus lowering the doctor:patient ratio from 1:2233 in 2001 to 1:1992. It also states that the number of nurses per 100,000 population rose from 76 in 2000 to 84 in 2001 and 2002. Although the ratios were much lower in the North-East the disparities are not highlighted in the bulletin. In Jaffna in 2002 there were 61 nurses per 100,000 population; in Mannar 38, in Vavuniya 49, in Batticaloa 66, in Amparai 34 and in Trincomalee 39. In Kilinochchi and Mullaitivu the rate was 8, the lowest in the country. In 2002 the number of medical officers per 100,000 population nationally was 49, in Jaffna the figure was 24, in Mannar 13, in Vavuniya 25, in Batticaloa 21, in Amparai 19 and in Trincomalee 26. In Kilinochchi and Mullaitivu the rate was as low as two. Mannar had one dental surgeon per 100,000 population, and Kilinochchi and Mullaitivu together had only one. As the bulletin showed, Kilinochchi, Mullaitivu and Mannar did not have a single medical specialist in 2002.

Table 22 Number of nurses and family health workers trained, 1991-2001

Year	Batticaloa		Jaffna	
	Nurses	**FHWs**	**Nurses**	**FHWs**
1991	24	07	0	49
1992	100	0	115	08
1993	27	0	30	27
1994	76	33	29	0
1995	24	0	0	0
1996	17	0	0	0
1997	0	30	0	0
1998	66	21	27	04
1999	11	91	0	0
2000	152	0	33	23
2001	57	0	01	11
2002	63	0	61	0

Sources: Sivarajah 2001, Sri Lanka Government 2002

7.4 Medical supplies

Ministry of Defense control; restriction of medicines and equipment; lack of medicines, consumable and equipment; working against the odds

Medical supplies include drugs, dressings, X-ray supplies and surgical consumables and nonconsumables. Strict procedures and rigid controls on such supplies, introduced by successive governments since 1992, have adversely affected the functioning of health institutions in the North-East. Requests for medical supplies are made to the Medical Supplies Division of the Department of Health Services by the Deputy Provincial Director of Health Services in the form of an annual list, divided into four quarter-periods. The lists from the northern region are also given to the ICRC. Medicines not available in the State Pharmaceutical Corporation or medicines that are banned are deleted from the lists. They are then sent to the Ministry of Defense, which makes the final decision on the quantities of medicines and equipment authorized for the region (in other areas the final decision on medicines and equipment is made by the Medical Supplies Division). Before the ceasefire, medicines approved by the Ministry of Defense for Jaffna and provided by the State Pharmaceutical Corporation were trucked to Trincomalee, where they were checked by naval officers and sent by an ICRC ship to Jaffna. Medicines to the Vanni and LTTE-controlled areas in the east were sent by lorry and checked at the crossing points into LTTE territory. In Jaffna, the unloaded medicines were checked again by the military before being sent to hospitals.

The Ministry of Defense usually cut the amount of medicines drastically without any consideration for actual needs. Around 20% of the medicines that are received have very short expiry periods. The opening of boxes of medicines several times en route and the resulting exposure to high temperatures and sunlight has damaged the effectiveness of the drugs, and nearly 12-15% have been stolen or damaged. The expenditure on medical supplies for Jaffna Teaching Hospital increased only by 4% from 1991 to 1992, but by 50% for other teaching hospitals in southern Sri Lanka (Natchinarkinian 1995) (see Table 23).

Table 23 Expenditure on medical supplies to teaching hospitals, 1990-1992*

Teaching hospital	Number of beds	Expenditure on medical supplies				
		1990	1991	% increase	1992	% increase
Colombo	5,250	77	167	116.8	272	62.9
Ragama	1,084	14	28	100.0	43	53.6
Kandy/Peradeniya	2,070	22	56	154.5	84	50.0
Galle	1,093	19	43	126.3	67	55.8
Jaffna	1,060	4‡	25	525‡	26	4.0

Notes: * Expenditure in LKR, millions
‡ The Jaffna hospital was in fact closed in 1990 due to bombing.
Source: 'Current pattern of health care and resource allocation' by Dr. C. S. Natchinarkinian in Victims of war in Sri Lanka: a quest for health consensus - Medical Institute of Tamils (UK), Tamil Information Centre (UK) and Tamil Refugee Relief Organization (US) 1995

In 1991, medical supplies were non-existent outside Point Pedro hospital where MSF worked, and Jaffna General Hospital was kept open by the ICRC. A solitary pharmacy remained open in Jaffna town (BRC 1991a). Sri Lankan human rights NGOs reported that throughout 1993 a lack of access to health supplies continued to cause serious problems in the north, with difficulties in the maintenance of health facilities and shortages of essential drugs and equipment (L & ST 1993).

The government continued to deny medical supplies to the North-East. In 1996 the Defense Ministry denied an ICRC request for medicines for its eight mobile clinics in the Vanni. Only 48 of the 101 medicines requested for Mullaitivu were allowed (BRC 1996a). In 1997, NGOs reported that drug quotas continued to be cut and transport delayed. Almost a third of the drugs which should have been sent to hospitals in LTTE areas in the last quarter of 1997 were not received until March 1998. Only 20-25% of the anti-malaria drugs due in the first quarter of 1998 had been received by mid-May. NGOs expressed concern that there was an acute shortage of anti-rabies vaccines and drugs to treat cholera. In hospitals in government-controlled Jaffna, there were often shortages of intravenous fluids and drugs (Save the Children 1998).

Of the applications for supplies for Jaffna for 2001, the Ministry of Defense refused approval of 21 items of medicines and medical equipment, and cut the quantity of 23 items by 25% of the amount requested and the quantity of 19 items by more than 50%. Approval was denied for X-ray developer, immunoglobin, heparin, eye drops, bandages, hydrogen peroxide, skin creams, surgical blades and other essentials. The following were cut by 25% or to below 50%: X-ray film, many essential drugs including antibiotics, vitamins, surgical spirit, sanitary pads and oxygen cylinders. The Colombo-based Consortium of Humanitarian Agencies reported that the embargo on so-called war-related items had further affected the welfare of the population, and that medical supplies were subject to embargoes, delays and shortages (CHA 2001).

In 2001 only 50-55% of hospital patients received the medicines they needed, and people suffering from chronic illnesses such as diabetes, arthritis, cancer, kidney failure and asthma did not receive regular medications. Patients requiring urgent major surgery suffered due to a lack of theatre facilities: some operations were conducted under local anaesthesia only and the ICRC transferred some patients to Colombo for surgery. Oxygen cylinders were retained at the Palaly military base and only 10 cylinders were provided at a time to major hospitals. During emergencies Jaffna General Hospital staff spent four or five hours travelling to and from the military base 25 km away to obtain oxygen cylinders. Pregnant women were denied vital drugs and injections such as anti-tetanus, ergometrine, tranquillizers and antibiotics. There was a severe shortage of glucose strips, sanitary pads, gauze, surgical spirit, adhesive plasters, antibiotics and medicines required for surgery. People suffering from kidney failure could not undergo haemodialysis when dialysers or solutions were not available and patients in a critical condition were treated with peritoneal dialysis. Essential drugs for psychiatric patients were grossly inadequate or not available.

The laboratory facilities in Jaffna General Hospital were poor, lacking modern facilities for microbiological studies, and there was no pathologist. Samples for biopsy, sera and viral studies were sent to Colombo and results arrived after long delays that sometimes proved fatal. Malnutrition and anaemic conditions among children and pregnant women were common due to inadequate diets, vitamins and iron supplements. The Defense Ministry cut anti-tetanus injections by 75%.

By 2008, the limited number of staff available to care for routine cases alongside war casualties had become a critical issue for several hospitals. The lack of regular deliveries of supplies had led to facilities in the Vanni running out of basic medicines such as paracetamol, antibiotics and vaccines (ICRC 2008).

8 The way forward

8.1 Conclusions

This evidence-based report analyzes, from a human rights and public health perspective, the impact of the violent conflict in Sri Lanka on health, the health system, and relief and reconstruction. Health is harmed by conflict-related damage to health-sustaining infrastructure and to the health system, as well as the corrosive effects of conflict-related factors such as poverty, unemployment, disrupted education, low morale and limited movement of people and supplies. The effects of war are usually measured by death and injuries due to weaponry, and the totals in Sri Lanka are likely to be at least a quarter of a million deaths and hundreds of thousands of trauma-related injuries. Less attention is usually paid to deaths and illnesses arising from the indirect effects of conflict, but as this report outlines, the longer-term impact on the population of the North-East has probably been equally dramatic.

Our examination of the health of the population in the northern and eastern regions of Sri Lanka suggests that a wide range of factors have had a major and negative impact on health. These include:

- 25 years of violent conflict;
- an economic embargo;
- continuous population displacement;
- human rights violations by all parties in the conflict;
- inadequate health facilities;
- shortages of staff, medicines and medical equipment;
- harassment of humanitarian workers and agencies;
- use of humanitarian aid as a weapon of war;
- Deliberate discrimination on ethnic grounds.

The Sri Lankan constitution guarantees freedom of movement but this right has been severely curtailed for the country's Tamil population, particularly in the North-East. Checkpoints, restricted zones, military camps and prohibited areas have affected all aspects of life and eroded rights, including the right to health. Agents of the state, including the police and the army, have continued to attack human rights defenders (including health workers) through murder, disappearances, assaults, injury, torture and death threats.

The Sri Lankan state and a succession of governments have violated human rights and undermined the rule of law. People cannot exercise their legitimate rights and carry on their daily lives with freedom and dignity. Security forces and groups aligned to the government have been involved in extra-judicial killings, illegal detention, torture, disappearances and rape. Some medical personnel have been implicated in torture and others have turned a blind eye to torture and degrading treatment. Successive governments have failed to take adequate measures to curb violations, compensate victims of abuse or punish the perpetrators, and have thus encouraged impunity. They have also introduced or maintained draconian legislation such as the Prevention of Terrorism Act and Emergency Regulations, in force for more than 30 years despite international concern, and used almost exclusively against the Tamil community.

Military operations have caused large-scale displacement of the Tamil population in the North-East. The government has applied considerable pressure to humanitarian agencies and many have been forced to leave the region and in some cases the country. Access to internally displaced persons and freedom of movement for civilians, humanitarian agency staff and relief supplies are among the most prominent challenges confronting aid agencies.

Sri Lanka has received praise for its achievements in improving health. Such assessments are partly based on statistics provided by the government, but these often contain inaccurate or misleading information on health in the North-East; demographic and health surveys have often excluded the conflict zones. The data scrutinized in this report, including detailed situation analyses from a range of sources, reflect the impact of the conflict. There are wide inequalities between people in the North-East and elsewhere in Sri Lanka, and between internally displaced people and the rest of the population. The infant mortality rate in the North-East, for example, is much higher than the island-wide average. Maternal deaths have been falling in the rest of the country, but increasing in the North-East. Nutritional surveys of children under 5 show a similar pattern. The lack of basic facilities and support has impeded the delivery of preventive and curative care, contributing to inequalities in the rates of malaria and other diseases.

The conflict and associated trauma have created huge psychological problems. Psychological disturbances are more common in displaced families. Repeated displacement and disruption of livelihoods have made people dependent on handouts. Women who have had to bear extra responsibilities without adequate support are particularly vulnerable.

Shortages of food and medicine have severely affected vulnerable people in the North-East, including the elderly, the disabled, widows, people traumatized by war and the tsunami, children and IDPs. In 2007, some districts were classified by the World Food Programme as being in 'acute food and livelihood crisis' owing to armed conflict and the government embargo on fuel, agricultural and construction materials. Jaffna and Batticaloa districts, classified as a 'humanitarian emergency', faced a widespread high-intensity conflict with thousands of IDPs, collapsing markets and increasing malnutrition.

Public health infrastructure and health care facilities, goods and services are not available in sufficient quantity or quality, including safe drinking water, adequate sanitation, health institutions, trained staff and essential drugs. The quality of health services is far below the rest of the island. Medicines received from Colombo are often out of date. Security forces were directly responsible for destroying many institutions, while others were closed for lack of staff and drugs or for security reasons. By 2002, 56 out of 405 health institutions in the North-East had been destroyed and 51 were not functioning. Hospitals and health centres are dilapidated and deteriorating.

The international community has responded with humanitarian assistance to North-East Sri Lanka, despite the government's failure to create a safe humanitarian space in which they can operate. The 51 nations and 22 international agencies that participated in the 2003 Tokyo Conference on Reconstruction and Development of Sri Lanka pledged $4.5 billion in aid for reconstruction. The conference co-chairs - Japan, the US, the European Union and Norway - were appointed to monitor and review progress in the peace process. Yet this process is regularly disrupted by renewed outbreaks of fighting, with both parties to the conflict accused of ignoring ceasefire agreements.

This report highlights the failure of all sides in the conflict to protect health, or to facilitate the rebuilding of a health system. . It describes the devastating direct and indirect impacts of the conflict particularly for those living in the area but also for Sri Lanka as a whole.

Conflict, criminality, social inequality, lack of democratic processes, political instability and decrepit essential infrastructure combine to damage health and arrest the development of a decentralized, primary care-based health system. Immediate action is needed: the need to find alternatives to violence and to resolve political differences peacefully, not least so that ordinary people can rebuild their shattered lives and health, could not be more urgent.

8.2 Recommendations

The Tamil Information Centre, deeply concerned by the conclusions of this report, makes the following recommendations:

(1) We call upon the Sri Lankan government, the LTTE leadership and the international community to take urgent measures to address the humanitarian crisis in North-East Sri Lanka; to ensure that the whole population receives adequate food, fuel, medical supplies and supplies for agriculture, industry and fisheries; and to provide IDPs with shelter and security.

Recommendations to the government of Sri Lanka

(2) We urge the government of Sri Lanka to end immediately the economic blockade of the northern and eastern regions and allow the supply of all materials needed for education, health, sanitation and economic activity.

(3) We urge the government of Sri Lanka to end the pursuit of a military solution, and to take measures to resolve the political deadlock, including discussions on substantial devolution of power to the North-East region on the basis of the Oslo Declaration of 2002.

(4) We urge the government of Sri Lanka to end all discrimination based on race, ethnicity or any other grounds and ensure that all people, including the population of the North-East, enjoy the right to life, health and other human rights, including:
access to adequate food, clean water, housing, employment, education, and health facilities; the right to human dignity, equality, privacy, freedom of information, association, assembly and movement the right to benefit from scientific progress and its applications.

(5) We urge the government of Sri Lanka to remove restrictions on the freedom of movement, to enable people to engage freely in social and economic activities, and to gain access to health facilities.

(6) We urge the government of Sri Lanka to make available to people in the North-East adequate and functioning public health and healthcare facilities, goods and services; and to provide adequate funds to rebuild, repair or refurbish existing facilities.

Recommendations to the international community

Considering that the right to health is dependent on, and contributes to, the realization of many other human rights,

(7) We call on the UN and the international community to continue to press for access by an international human rights monitoring body to all parts of Sri Lanka and relevant institutions, with a view to improving human rights and ensuring all actors in Sri Lanka observe their human rights obligations and commitments.

(8) We call on the UN and the international community to ensure that a mechanism for the investigation of human rights violations throughout the island is established, with international participation, which meets the requirements of independence, credibility, effectiveness and empowerment, and thus contributes to public confidence, peace and stability in all parts of Sri Lanka.

(9) We call on the UN and the international community to ensure that impunity (exemption from punishment or loss) for state officials and members of the security forces is ended in Sri Lanka, paying special attention to the laws and regulations that contribute to impunity, particularly through proper, impartial investigations of alleged torture, rape, disappearances and extra-judicial executions; and that all perpetrators, irrespective of ethnic origin, position or status, are prosecuted.

(10) We call on the UN and the international community to urge the Sri Lankan government to recognize the role of human rights defenders in the protection of human rights and fundamental freedoms; to end all verbal and physical attacks on human rights defenders; and to promote a mechanism for the protection of human rights defenders so they can carry out their work unimpeded.

(11) We call on the UN, the EU, the Co-Chairs of the Conference on Reconstruction and Development of Sri Lanka (held in Tokyo, June 2003), governments and all other relevant bodies to exert greater pressure on the Sri Lankan government and the Liberation Tigers of Tamil Eelam (LTTE) to return to the negotiating table and continue negotiations until a political settlement is reached.

Recommendations to UN organizations working on health

Considering that discrimination in access to health services based on race has continued in Sri Lanka for several decades:

(12) We request the World Health Organization (WHO), other relevant UN bodies and international agencies to review as necessary, and ensure implementation of their policies and programmes in relation to Sri Lanka, in order to avoid discrimination and ensure that all people are treated equally and have equal access to health facilities.

(13) We request the UN Special Rapporteur on the right to the highest attainable standard of physical and mental health, and the Special Rapporteur on the right to food, to investigate discrimination in these areas in Sri Lanka, and the UN Human Rights Council to take appropriate measures based on their findings.

(14) We request WHO, other relevant UN bodies and international agencies to facilitate the study of the impact of war on health in Sri Lanka, so that research can be carried out in the affected regions as a basis for planning and the provision of greater assistance to these regions.

(15) We request WHO, other relevant UN bodies and international agencies to urge the Sri Lankan government to enable the training of more specialists in forensic medicine and in human rights promotion, and to ensure protection for doctors and specialists in these areas.

Appendix

Government restrictions on materials to northern Sri Lanka, 2001

Materials needing permits from the Defence Ministry or Vavuniya army headquarters

1. Vehicles including motor cycle
2. Electricity generators
3. Water pumps with electric motors
4. Batteries for vehicles
5. Outboard motors for boats and diving equipment
6. Fibre
7. Typewriters
8. Copying (cyclostyle) machines
9. Photocopiers
10. Printing machines
11. Video equipment
12. Cameras
13. Surgical equipment
14. Medicines in large quantities
15. Fertilizers
16. Agro-chemicals and Other chemicals
17. Aluminium and aluminium-made objects
18. Kerosene (paraffin) in large quantities

Materials allowed in small quantities with permission from Vavuniya army headquarters

Food

19. Instant noodles
20. Canned fruit
21. Fruit juice cartons and cordials
22. Powdered fruit drinks
23. Soup cubes
24. Gelatin powder
25. Biscuit packets (below 250gms)
26. Tinned cheese
27. Glucose
28. Canned fish (below 250gms)

Vehicle needs

29. All kinds of grease and lubricants
30. Motor mechanic spanners and other related equipment
31. Tyres, tubes and other spare parts for bicycles

Printing needs

32. Photocopying paper
33. Maps, and paper for maps
34. Newsprint
35. Paper for copying (cyclostyle) machines
36. Printing ink and ink copying machines
37. Bristle board
38. Unlined foolscap paper

Other materials

39. Building materials
40. Sacks, polythene and polythene bags
41. Resins
42. Jerry cans and other cans
43. Buckets (above 5 litre capacity)
44. Agricultural implements (hoes, crowbars etc.)

Medicines allowed to a person with a prescription

45. Medicines issued to a patient released from government hospital (letter from hospital necessary)
46. Medicines issued to a patient released from government hospital supported by a prescription

Medicines allowed to a person without a prescription

47. Forty eight aspirin tablets
48. Two medium sized bottles of balm
49. Two medium sized bottles of syrup
50. Thirty vitamin tablets or capsules
51. Sixty malaria tablets

Other materials allowed to a person without a permit

52. Forty kilograms of food

When official health statistics fall silent

The Sri Lankan Health Bulletin is published annually, but data often excludes the North-East or districts within the North-Eastern. However, it is the health of these populations that has been most affected by the direct and indirect consequences of war. This exclusion disguises the disparities and gives favorable key indicators, such as infant and maternal mortality, for Sri Lanka in comparison with other countries. For example, Annual Health Bulletin 2002 nation-wide data on key aspects excludes the North-East Province:

Demography

- 'Population of Sri Lanka by age & sex 1981 & 2001'
Fig 1.2 – excludes Northern and Eastern Provinces

- **'Sex ratio of population 1871-2001'**
Table 1.1 - 1994 and 2001 data exclude Northern and Eastern Provinces

- **'Literacy rate by sex 1881-1994'**
Table 1.7 – 1994 and 2001 data exclude Northern and Eastern Provinces

- **'Percentage of distribution of population 2001'**
Table 1.8 – excludes Northern and Eastern Provinces

- **'Size of population and number of medical officers of health'**
on page 15 – excludes Northern and Eastern Provinces

- **'Population by five year age groups and sex 1981 and 2001'**
Table 3 – 2001 data excludes Jaffna, Mannar, Vavuniya, Mullaitivu, Kilinochchi, Batticaloa and Trincomalee districts

Infrastructure

- **'Number of health institutions and hospital beds 1975-2002'**
Table 2.1 - 1990 data excludes Northern and Eastern provinces; 1995 data excludes Jaffna, Kilinochchi, Mullaitivu and Amprai districts

Sanitation and Water Supply

- **'Percentage distribution of housing units by source of drinking water, 2001'**
Table 5 — excludes Northern and Eastern Provinces

- **'Percentage distribution of housing units by type of toilet, 2001'**
Table 6 — excludes Northern and Eastern Provinces

Hospital In Patient and Out Patient Activities

- **'Trends in in-patient and out-patient attendance and rate per 1,000 population 1960-2002'**
Table 4.1 - 1990 data excludes the Northern and Eastern provinces; 1995 data excludes Jaffna, Kilinochchi and Amparai districts; 1996 data excludes Kilinochchi and Mullaitivu districts; 1997 data excludes Amparai district

- **'In-patient and out-patient attendance in government medical institution 1966-2002'**
Figure 4.1 – 1990 and 1991 data exclude Northern and Eastern Provinces; 1994 data excludes Jaffna, Kilinochchi, Mullaitivu and Amparai districts; 1995 data excludes Kilinochchi and Mullativu districts; 1996 data excludes Amparai disctrict

- **'Leading causes of hospitalization 1995-2002'**
Table 23 - 1995 data excludes Jaffna, Mullaitivu and Amparai districts; 1996 data excludes Kilinochchi and Mullaitivu districts; 1997 data excludes Amparai district; 2002 excludes Kilinochchi district

- **'Average duration of stay in selected types of hospitals 1965-2002'**
Table 34 - 1990 data excludes Northern and Eastern provinces; 1995 data excludes Jaffna, Kilinochchi, Mullaitivu and Amparai districts

Live Births and Deaths

- **'All registered births including hospital births 1960-2002'**
Table 35 - 1990 and 1991 data exclude Northern and Eastern provinces; 1996 and 1997 data exclude Kilinochchi and Mullaitivu districts

- **'Percentage of live births and deaths in government hospitals 1966-2002'**
Figure 4.2 - 1990 and 1991 data exclude Northern and Eastern provinces; 1994 data excludes Jaffna, Kilinochchi, Mullaitivu and Amparai districts; 1995 data excludes Kilinochchi and Mullaitivu districts; 1996 data excludes Amparai district

Morbidity and Mortality

- **'Trends in hospital morbidity by broad disease groups 1980-2002'**
Table 19 - figures for 1990 exclude Northern and Eastern provinces and figures for 1995 exclude Jaffna, Kilinochchi, Mullaitivu and Amparai districts

- **'Trends in hospitalization and hospital deaths of selected diseases 1975-2002'**
Table 20 - figures for 1990 exclude Northern and Eastern provinces and figures for 1995 exclude Jaffna, Kilinochchi, Mullaitivu and Amparai districts

- **'Morbidity and mortality of diarrhoeal diseases and case fatality rates 1980-2002'**
Table 53 - figures for 1990 and 1991 exclude the Northern and Eastern provinces; figures for 1995 exclude Jaffna, Kilinochchi, Mullaitivu and Amparai districts; figures for1997 exclude Amparai district; figures for 2002 exclude Kilinochchi district

- **'Morbidity and mortality of Shigellosis and case fatality rates 1980-2002'**
Table 54 - figures for 1990 and 1991 exclude the Northern and Eastern provinces; the 1995 figures exclude Jaffna, Kilinochchi, Mullaitivu and Amparai districts; the 1997 figures exclude Amparai district; figures for 2002 exclude Kilinochchi district

- **'Leading causes on hospital deaths 1995-2002'**
Table 26 - figures for 1996 exclude Kilinochchi, Mullaitivu and Amparai districts; figures for 1997 exclude Amparai District; figures for 2006 exclude Kilinochchi district

- **'Leading causes of hospital deaths 2002'**
Table 24 - excludes Kilinochchi district

- **'Leading causes of hospital deaths by district 2002'**
Table 25 - excludes Kilinochchi district

- **'Cases of deaths of poisoning and case fatality rate 2002'**
Table 27 – excludes Kilinochchi district

- **'Distribution of mental disorders by region/campaign 2002'**
Table 28 - excludes Kilinochchi district

- **'Case fatality rate for selected diseases 1985'**
Table 33 - excludes Kilinochchi district

- **'In-patients treated and hospital deaths by types of institution and district 2002'**
Table 37 – excludes Kilinochchi district

- **'Distribution of modifiable diseases by district 2002'**
Table 44 - excludes Kilinochchi district

References

Ali A (1997). The Muslim factor in the Sri Lankan ethnic crisis. Journal of Muslim Minority Affairs, October, 17:2.

Amnesty International
- (1984). Sri Lanka: Current human rights concerns and evidence of extrajudicial killings by the security forces, July 1983-April 1984, Document ASA 37/05/84.
- (1985). Annual report.
- (1987). Extrajudicial killings/'Disappearances' – Sri Lanka: 150 civilians, ASA 37/02/876.
- (1992). Sri Lanka: Summary of human rights concerns during 1991, ASA 37/01/92.
- (1994). Sri Lanka: Summary of human rights concerns, ASA 37/09/94, February.
- (1995). Sri Lanka: Appeal for full implementation of commitment to human rights. ASA 37/15/95.
- (1996). Sri Lanka: Further information on extra-judicial killings, ASA 37/05/96.
- (2006). Sri Lanka: Amnesty International condemns killings of civilians, 16 May (www.amnesty.org/en/library/asset/ASA37/014/2006/en/dom-ASA370142006en.html).
- (2008a). Sri Lanka: Fears for civilians increase as war intensifies, ASA 37/022/2007, 15 July (www.amnesty.org/en/library/info/ASA37/022/2008/en).
- (2008b). Sri Lanka: Blocking aid workers endangers trapped civilians, 9 September (www.amnesty.org/en/for-media/press-releases/sri-lanka-blocking-aid-workers-endangers-trapped-civilians-20080909)
- (2008c). Sri Lanka: Hundreds of thousands trapped in the Wanni need urgent shelters, 19 November.

Aravinthan M (2003). Sri Lanka: displaced Jaffna refugees want military zones dismantled, 7 July (www.wsws.org/articles/2003/jul2003/jaff-j07.shtml).

Asian Development Bank (2005). Asian Development Outlook 2005 - Sri Lanka (www.adb.org/documents/books/ADO/2005/sri.asp).

Asian Development Bank, United Nations and World Bank (2003). Sri Lanka: assessment of needs in the conflict affected areas of the North-East (www.peaceinsrilanka.org/Downloads/Assessment%20of%20Needs1.pdf).

Asian Human Rights Commission
- (2000). Crime Against Humanity - Sri Lanka: systematic detention, torture, rape and murder as weapon of war (www.ahrchk.net/ua/mainfile.php/2000/372/).
- (2006). Sri Lanka: Abductions and disappearances continue in Colombo and elsewhere unabated and the state turns a blind eye (www.ahrchk.net/statements/mainfile.php/2006statements/859/).
- (2008). Sri Lanka: Internal repression internationally condemned (www.ahrchk.net/statements/mainfile.php/2008statements/1546/).

British Medical Association (2007). The right to health: a toolkit for health professionals (p22) (www.bma.org.uk/ap.nsf/Content/Righttohealthtoolkit).

British Refugee Council. Articles in Sri Lanka Monitor (April 1996-March 2004 articles may be accessed at http://breslproject.gn.apc.org/index.html).
- (1990a). Battered Jaffna on the brink of starvation; 100,000 flee the North-East, August
- (1990b). Killing spree continues in Batticaloa, September.
- (1990c). New army offensive jolts Jaffna: Tigers expel Muslims from the North, October.
- (1991a). The road to Jaffna, February.
- (1991b). Trincomalee boils over, March.

- (1991c). Gunning down the Good Samaritan, April.
- (1991d). Massacre of the innocents, June.
- (1992). Painkiller. April.
- (1993a). Civilians die in air attack, August.
- (1993b). 100,000 families hit by fishing ban, September.
- (1993c). LTTE declares 1994 a year of battles, December.
- (1994). A child dies, December.
- (1995a). Massacre, Sri Lanka Monitor, July.
- (1995b). Licensing atrocity, September.
- (1996a). The spoils of war. March.
- (1996b). Jaffna amid the ruins, April.
- (1996c). Living in Jaffna. June.
- (1996d). Hospital deaths, August.
- (1996e). Kilinochchi standoff: 200,000 refugees struggle in the Vanni, August.
- (1997a). Relief slashed for refugees, April.
- (1997b). Battle for the Vanni, May.
- (1997c). Bureaucrats slash food aid, June.
- (1997d). Denying basic needs, July.
- (1997e). Refugee children die in Mannar, July.
- (1997f). Refugees die in air attack, August.
- (1997g). Hidden casualties, August.
- (1997h). Protection denied, November.
- (1998a). Health crisis, January.
- (1998b). Refugees hit by food cuts, August.
- (1998c). Food aid to the north slashed, June.
- (1998d). Appeal to the UN over food cuts, November.
- (1998e). Fishing ban, November.
- (1998f) Health crisis, December.
- (1999a). Food problems, May.
- (1999b). Sunny village sacked, July.
- (1999c). Humanitarian crisis, July.
- (1999d). Agreement on Vanni route, Sri Lanka Monitor, August.
- (1999e). Food aid weapon, Briefing, October.
- (1999f). NGOs appeal to the UN, October.
- (1999g). Supply route, November.
- (1999h). Health risks, November.
- (2000a). Food aid to Vanni reduced, January.
- (2000b) LTTE prisoners protest, February.
- (2000c). Children killed, May.
- (2001a). Death from the skies, March.
- (2001b). Medical crisis, April.
- (2001c). Displacement ordeal, June.
- (2002). STF kill seven civilians, October.

British Refugee Council
- (2001d). Sri Lanka: Human rights and return of refugees, Sri Lanka Project, December (http://repository.forcedmigration.org/show_metadata.jsp pid=fmo:2769).
- (2003). Sri Lanka: Internally displaced persons and safe returns, Sri Lanka Project, september (www.refugeecouncil.org.uk/OneStopCMSCore/).

Centre for Policy Alternatives (2007). Policy brief on humanitarian issues, December (http://www.cpalanka.org/Policy_Brief/Brief_on_Humanitarian_Issues.pdf).

Chase R, Bush K (2001). The Mental Health of War Affected Children: a Community-based Rehabilitation and Reconciliation Programme in Sri Lanka's Eastern Province (www.humanities.mcmaster.ca/peace-health/Conf2001/chasbush.pdf).

Christian Aid (1998). Health Crisis Forgotten as Prince Charles Visits Sri Lanka, statement, 2 February.

Consortium of Humanitarian Agencies (2001). Situation report July/August 2001, CHA Newsletter.

Egeland, Jan (2006). UN Under-Secretary-General for Humanitarian Affairs and Emergency Relief Coordinator Statement - 18 October 2006 (http://www.humanitarianinfo.org/srilanka/catalogue/Files/Media%20Centre/Press%20Centre/PC_061018%20%20United%20Nations%20Surveys%20Northern%20Sri%20Lanka.pdf).

Engineering Consultancy Bureau, Jaffna (1991). Assessment of the war damage in the city of Jaffna. Study commissioned by the Jaffna Municipal Commissioner, November.

European Union
- (2005). Statement at the Sri Lanka Development Forum, Kandy, 16-17 May (http://www.dellka.ec.europa.eu/).
- (2008). EU calls for humanitarian workers to be safeguarded in Sri Lanka, 7 January (www.dellka.ec.europa.eu/en/whatsnew/2008/html/PR-080107-2.htm).

Food and Agricultural Organization (1997). Special report on crop and food supply assessment mission to Sri Lanka, 9 April (www.fao.org).

Free Media Movement (2007). Sri Lanka: killing and disappearance of 57 humanitarian workers reported, 6 September (http://www.freemediasrilanka.org/English/news.php/id=43§ion=news_reports).

Good A (2003). Report on the fact-finding visit to Sri Lanka, 2-15 August 2003, University of Edinburgh, UK.

Hafez G (1998). Maternal mortality: a neglected and socially unjustifiable tragedy: why WHO selected 'Safe motherhood' as the slogan for World Health Day 1998, Eastern Mediterranean Health Journal, 4, 1 (www.emro.who.int/publications/emhj/0401/03.htm).

Human Development Centre (2006). Report of August 2006 from Jaffna.

Human Rights Watch
- (1992). Abdication of responsibility: The Commonwealth and Human Rights, October (www.hrw.org/reports).
- (1999a) Closure threatens civilians in Sri Lanka, 8 February (www.hrw.org/en/news/1999/08/01/closure-threatens-civilians-sri-lanka/print).
- (1999b). Parties must reach agreement on humanitarian access, 2 August (www.hrw.org).
- (2001). World Report 2001: Sri Lanka (www.humanrightswatch.org/wr2k1/asia/srilanka.html).
- (2002). World Report 2002: Sri Lanka (www.hrw.org/legacy/wr2k2/asia10.html).

- (2007). Return to war: Human rights under siege, August (www.hrw.org/en/reports/2007/08/05/return-war).
- (2009). War on the displaced: Sri Lanka army and LTTE abuses against civilians in the Vanni, 20 February 2009 (www.hrw.org/en/reports/2009/02/19/war-displaced)
Indrapala K (2005). The evolution of an ethnic identity: the Tamils in Sri Lanka c.300 BCE to c.1200 CE, The South Asian Studies Centre, Sydney.

INFORM (1993). The human rights situation in Sri Lanka 1993, Sri Lanka Information Monitor, Colombo.

Institute of Peace and Conflict Studies (2007). High Security Zones in Sri Lanka (http://www.ipcs.org/whatsNewArticle11.jsp/action=showView&kValue-2337&status=article&mod=b).

Integrated Food Security Programme
- (1999). Baseline survey health and nutrition, Trincomalee, Working Paper 24, Reinhard I, Kramer D (http://www.ifsp-srilanka.org/html/wp_24_baseline_survey_health_a.html).
- (2000). Conflict mitigation through food security, Geinitz D, Reinhard I (http://www.ifsp-srilanka.org/wp-36-conflict-mitigation.pdf).

Internal Displacement Monitoring Centre
- (2006). Severely restricted humanitarian access and serious security threat to aid community (www.internal-displacement.org/idmc/website/countries.nsf/(httpEnvelopes)/).
- (2008a). Returns in the east but new displacements in the north (www.internal-displacement.org/8025708F004CE90B/(httpCountrySummaries)/).
- (2008b). Sri Lanka: IDPs around Colombo must register again, IDP News Alert, 25 September (www.internal-displacement.org/8025708F004D31AA/(httpIDPNewsAlerts)/).

International Campaign to Ban Landmines
- Landmine Monitor Reports 2001-2006
- (2003). Towards a mine-free world, Landmine Monitor Report 2003 (http://www.icbl.org/lm/2003/sri_lanka.html).
- (2007). Landmine Monitor Report 2007 (http://www.icbl.org/lm/2007/sri_lanka.html).

International Commission of Jurists (2006). Letter to President Mahinda Rajapakse from Nicholas Howen, ICJ Secretary General, dated 5 September.

International Committee of the Red Cross (2008). Sri Lanka: Several hospitals in northern Sri Lanka face increasing challenges, 17 April (www.icrc.org).

International Freedom of Expression Exchange (2006). International mission finds deteriorating security situation for media, report of mission 9-11 October (http://www.ifex.org/en/content/view/full/78466/).

International Independent Group of Eminent Persons (2007). Second public statement by P N Bhagwati, Chairman, 15 June (www.pchrv.gov.lk/news).

International Monetary Fund (IMF) (2007). IMF Country Report no 07/374 Sri Lanka: Selected Issues (http://www.imf.org/external/pubs/ft/scr/2007/cr07374.pdf).

Internatinoal Monetary Fund (IMF) (2008a). IMF Balance of Payments and International Investment Position Statistics, 24 July 2008 (http://www.imf.org/external/np/sta/bop/bop.htm).

International Monetary Fund (IMF) (2008b). IMF World Economic Outlook Database, October 2008, (http://www.imf.org/external/pubs/ft/weo/2008/02/weodata/index.aspx).

International Rehabilitation Council for Torture Victims (2004). Medical aspects of torture as seen in Sri Lanka, Denmark (http://www.irct.org/Files/Filer/publications/ipip/National-adaptation-Sri-Lanka-medical-material.pdf).

Jayasekera D (1999), Tamil plantation youth recount brutal torture by Sri Lankan police, 13 May (www.wsws.org/articles/1999/may1999/sri-m13.shtml).

Law and Society Trust
- (1993). Sri Lanka: State of human rights 1993. Sri Lanka.
- (1995). Sri Lanka: State of human rights 1995. Sri Lanka.
- (1998). Sri Lanka: State of human rights 1998. Sri Lanka.
- (2000). Sri Lanka: State of human rights 1999. Sri Lanka.
- (2001). Sri Lanka: State of human rights 2001. Sri Lanka.
- (2008a). Civil society solidarity with international humanitarian organizations, statement issued by 13 Sri Lankan human rights agencies, 18 January (www.lawandsocietytrust.org/PDF/).
- (2008b) Under fire - Persons in humanitarian service: Report on killings and disappearances of persons in humanitarian service in Sri Lanka January 2006-December 2007 (www.lawandsocietytrust.org).

Levy BS and Sidel VW (2008). War and Public Health, Oxford University Press, New York.

Médecins sans Frontières
- (2002). Psychological trauma of the civil war in Sri Lanka (de Jong K et.al.), 26 April (www.msf.org/msfinternational).
- (2007) Civilians increasingly under fire in Sri Lankan conflict, Activity Report 2007 (http://fieldresearch.msf.org/msf/bitstream/10144/18134/1/lancet%20de%20jong%20sri%20lanka.pdf).
- (2008). Sri Lanka conflict isolated MSF-assisted population, 28 January (http://www.msf.org.uk/Sri Lanka_Conflict_Isolates_MSFAssisted_Population_20080313.news).

Medical Foundation for the Care of Victims of Torture (2000). Caught in the middle: a study of Tamil torture survivors coming to the UK from Sri Lanka (Peel M, Salinsky M), London.

Medical Institute of Tamils (UK), Tamil Information Centre (UK) and Tamil Refugee Relief Organization (US) (eds) (1995), Victims of war in Sri Lanka: a quest for health consensus, London.

Natchinarkinian C (1995). Current pattern of health care and resource allocation. In: Medical Institute of Tamils (UK), Tamil Information Centre (UK) and Tamil Refugee Relief Organization (US) (eds), Victims of war in Sri Lanka: a quest for health consensus, London.

Obermeyer Z, Murray C, Gakidou E (2008). Fifty years of violent war deaths from Vietnam to Bosnia: analysis of data from the world health survey programme, British Medical Journal, 19 June (www.bmj.com).

Paust J (1998). The human rights to food, medicine and medical supplies, and freedom from arbitrary and inhuman detention and controls in Sri Lanka. Vanderbilt Journal of Transnational Law, 31, 3, May.

Perera J (2006). Opening the A9 highway can also open the road to peace, Daily Mirror (Sri Lanka), 7 November.

Press Emblem Campaign (2007). PEC Media Casualties 2007: A record year never witnessed before, 17 December, Geneva (www.pressemblem.ch).

Reporters sans Frontières (2008). Sri Lanka: Annual Report 2008 (http://www.rsf.org/article.php3?id_article=25690).

Reuters (2007). Sri Lanka rebukes UN aid chief over safety fears. Statement made to Reuters on 9 August by Sir John Holmes, UN Under Secretary General for Humanitarian Affairs, 10 August (http://uk.reuters.com).

Sarvananthan M
- (2002). Economic imperative for peace in Sri Lanka (http://www.satp.org/satporgtp/publication/fault-lines/volume15/Article2.htm).
- (2007). Economy of the conflict region in Sri Lanka: From embargo to repression, East-West Centre, Washington DC.

Save the Children UK (1998). Realizing Rights: Children affected by armed conflict in North and East Sri Lanka, Situation Report No.2.

Seneviratne U, Dissanayake S (2002). Neurological manifestations of snake bite in Sri Lanka, Journal of Postgraduate Medicine, 48, 4 (www.jpgmonline.com).

Sivarajah N (2001). Health care for North-East Sri Lanka: Reflections for the future, Thesam, London.

Somasundaram D
- (2002). Child soldiers: understanding the context, British Medical Journal, 324, 25 May (www.bmj.com/cgi/content/full/324/7348/1268).
- (2003). Addressing the psychosocial problems of women in a war ravaged society
- Department of Psychiatry, Faculty of Medicine, University of Jaffna, February (www.lines-magazine.org/Art Feb03/Daya.htm).
- (2008). Psycho-social aspects of torture in Sri Lanka, International Journal of Culture and Mental Health, 1, 1, June.

Sri Lanka Government
- (1976). Sri Lanka Nutritional Status Survey September 1975-March 1976, Ministry of Health, US Department of Health Education and Welfare and CARE Sri Lanka.
- (1985a). Emergency (Prohibited Zone) Regulations, Gazette, No. 332/23, 18 January.
- (1985b). Surveillance Zone regulations, Gazette, No. 341/36, 18 March.
- (1991). Gazette notification No. 674/16 of 9 August and No. 692/4 of 9 December.
- (1992). Emergency (Establishment of Prohibited Zone) Regulation, Gazette No. 736/17, 16 October.
- (1993a). Emergency (Establishment of Prohibited Zone) Regulation, Gazette No. 752/15, 1 Feb.
- (1993b). Emergency (Prohibition on use of boats) Regulation, Gazette No. 782/7, 1 September.
- (1993c). Emergency (Establishment of Prohibited Zone) Regulation, Gazette No. 784/20, 17 Sept.

- (2000). Annual Health Bulletin 2000, Department of Health Services (www.searo.who.int).
- (2001a). Annual Report 2001, Central Bank of Sri Lanka.
- (2001b). Notification of the Defence Secretary dated 2 August 2001 [Gazette No. 1195/18, 3 August] under Prevention of Terrorism (Restricted Articles) Regulations No. 9, 20 July [Government Gazette No. 1193/31, 21 July 2001].
- (2001c). Prevention of Terrorism (Prohibited Zone) Regulation No. 8 of 2001, Gazette No. 11931/31, 21 July.
- (2001d). Demographic and Health Survey 2000, Department of Census and Statistics.
- (2002a). Prevention of Terrorism Act (Restricted Zones) Regulation No. 1 of 23 May.
- (2002b). Annual Health Bulletin 2002, Department of Health Services.
- (2004) Consumer Finances and Socio-economic Survey 2003-2004, Central Bank of Sri Lanka (www.cbsl.lk).
- (2008a). Sri Lanka: Demographic and health survey 2006/7, Department of Census and Statistics and Ministry of Health Care and Nutrition (www.statistics.gov.lk).
- (2008b). Poverty indicators: Household income and expenditure survey 2006/7, Department of Census and Statistics and the Ministry of Finance and Planning.

Sri Lanka Supreme Court (2005). Decisions of 15 July and 21 November 2005.

Strategic Foresight (2006). Cost of conflict in Sri Lanka (www.strategicforesight.com).

Tambiah S (1986). Sri Lanka: Ethnic fratricide and dismantling of democracy, The University of Chicago Press.

Tamil Information Centre, UK
- (2005). Tsunami disaster situation report No. 3. TIC, London.
- (2006). The UN Human Rights Council must urge the Sri Lankan government to end restrictions on food, fuel and medicines to people of the North-East. Memorandum to the UN Human Rights Council, 23 November.
- (2008a). Sri Lanka: Submissions of the Tamil Information Centre to the Universal Periodic Review, UN Human Rights Council, 1 February 2008, May 2008 sessions.
- (2008b). Sri Lanka: Human rights situation demands robust international intervention. Submission to members of the UN Human Rights Council, March.

United Nations - press releases:
- (2000). 14 March 2000 (http://www.unhchr.ch/huricane/huricane.nsf/view01/27CD954D0E41F7D1802568A200622F69?opendocument).
- (2007). Special Rapporteur on Torture concludes visit to Sri Lanka, 29 October (http://www.unhchr.ch/huricane/huricane.nsf/view01/F493C88D3AFDCDBEC1257383006CD8BB?opendocument).
- (2008) United Nations expert group deplores recent wave of disappearances in Sri Lanka, 11 June (http://www.unhchr.ch/huricane/huricane.nsf/view01/D564F9EDD64E959FC12574650049042C?opendocument).
- (2008). Ban voices alarm at increased violence in northern Sri Lanka, 9 September (www.un.org/apps/news).

UN Committee against Torture
- (1998). Sri Lanka: Concluding observations, A/53/44, paras.243-257 (http://daccessdds.un.org/doc/UNDOC/GEN/N98).

- (2005). Sri Lanka: Conclusions and recommendations, CAT/CLKA/CO/2 (http://daccessdds.un.org/doc/UNDOC/GEN/G05/455/14/PDF/G0545514.pdf?OpenElement).

UN Committee on Economic, Social and Cultural Rights
- (1997). Report submitted by Sri Lanka, E/1990/5/Add.32 (http://daccessdds.un.org/doc/UNDOC/GEN/G97/150/63/PDF/).
- (1998). Concluding observations: Sri Lanka, E/C.12/1/Add.24, paragraph 7 (http://daccessdds.un.org/doc/UNDOC/GEN/G98/164/70/PDF/G9816470.pdf?OpenElement).
- (2000). The right to the highest attainable standard of health, 22nd Session, E/C.12/2000/4. (General Comments) (www.unhchr.ch/tbs/doc.nsf/(Symbol)/).

UNFPA (2008). State of World Population (www.unfpa.org).

UN High Commissioner for Refugees
- (2001). Refugee NewsNet (www.unhcr.ch/refworld).
- (2004-2007) Asylum levels and trends in industrialized countries, reports (www.unhcr.org).
- (2005). Sri Lanka: UNHCR Global Appeal 2005 (www.unhcr.org/publ/PUBL/41ab28ccc.pdf).
- (2008a). UNHCR deeply concerned about newly displaced in Sri Lanka's north, News Stories, 8 August (www.unhcr.org).
- (2008b). Eight Sri Lankan refugees drown while returning home, Briefing Notes, 16 September (www.unhcr.org).

UN Human Rights Commission
- (1987a). Statement of the Indian delegation before the Commission, 2 March.
- (1987b). Resolution 1987/61 adopted by the Commission, 12 March.
- (2005). Interdependence between democracy and human rights, report of second expert seminar Democracy and the rule of law, Geneva, 28 February-2 March, submitted to 61st Session, 18 March, E/CN.4/2005/58 (http://daccessdds.un.org/doc/UNDOC/GEN/).

UN Human Rights Committee (2003). Sri Lanka: Concluding observations, CCPR/CO/79/LKA (http://daccessdds.un.org/doc/UNDOC/GEN/G03/456/23/PDF/G0345623.pdf?OpenElement).

UN Human Rights Council (2006). Address of the UN High Commissioner for Human Rights, Louise Arbour, at the Second Session, 18 September (www.ohchr.org/english/bodies/hrcouncil).

UN Inter Agency Standing Committee (2008). Situation report 143, 4-11 September 2008 (www.reliefweb.int/rw/RWFiles2008.nsf/FilesByRWDocUnidFilename/FBUO-7JHFV4-full_report.pdf/$File/full_report.pdf).

UN Office for the Coordination of Humanitarian Affairs
- (2006). Sri Lanka situation reports 2006 (http.ochaonline.un.org).
- (2008a). Common Humanitarian Action Plan for Sri Lanka (CHAP).
- (2008b). Sri Lanka: Tough times continue for Jaffna residents, Integrated Regional Information Network (IRIN), 10 March (www.irinnews.org).
- (2008c). Sri Lanka: Food insecurity a growing problem, IRIN, 9 April (www.irinnews.org).
- (2008d). Sri Lanka: UN, NGOs to pull out from north, IRIN, 10 September (www.irinnews.org).
- (2008e). Sri Lanka: UN completes relocation from Tamil Tiger area, IRIN, 16 September (www.irinnews.org).

- (2008f). Sri Lanka: Children stunted, wasted, underweight - government health survey, 15 August (http://www.irinnews.org).

UN Office of the High Commissioner for Human Rights (2005). Sri Lanka: Conclusions and recommendations on report submitted by the State Party. CAT/C/LKA/CO/2 (www.unhchr.ch/tbs/doc.nsf/(Symbol)/CAT.C.LKA.CO.2.En?Opendocument).

UN Special Envoy for Tsunami Recovery (2005). Tsunami recovery: Taking stock after 12 months, Bill Clinton (www.tsunamispecialenvoy.org).
UN Special Rapporteur on Extrajudicial, Summary or Arbitrary Executions
- (1991). E/CN.4/1991/36 paras 471- 472.
- (1998). Bacre Waly Ndiaye, submitted to the UN Commission on Human Rights, 54th Session, following a visit to Sri Lanka, 12 March 1998. E/CN.4/1998/68/Add.2 (http://daccessdds.un.org/doc/UNDOC/GEN/G98/109/17/PDF/G9810917.pdf?OpenElement).
- (2006). Report of the mission to Sri Lanka 28 November to 6 December 2005, E/CN.4/2006/53/Add.5 (http://daccessdds.un.org/doc/UNDOC).

UN Special Rapporteur on Torture (2008). Manfred Nowak, report of mission to Sri Lanka 1-8 October 2007, A/HRC/7/3/Add.6 (http://daccessdds.un.org/doc/UNDOC/GEN/G08/111/35/PDF/G0811135.pdf?OpenElement).

UN Special Representative of the Secretary General on Human Rights Defenders (2004). Hina Jilani, 59th session of the UN General Assembly, 1 October, A/59/401 (http://daccessdds.un.org/doc/UNDOC/GEN/N04/533/18/PDF/N0453318.pdf?OpenElement).
- (2006). Independent experts express serious concern over the escalation of violence in Sri Lanka, 11 August, UN Office at Geneva (http://www.unog.ch/unog/website).

UN Special Representative of the Secretary-General on Internally Displaced Persons (2008). Walter Kälin, mission to Sri Lanka from 14-21 December 2007, A/HRC/8/6/Add.4 – paragraph 16 (e).

UN Special Representative of the Secretary General on Internally Displaced Persons (1994), UN Human Rights Commission (1994). E/CN.4/1994/44/Add.1 (http://daccessdds.un.org/doc/UNDOC/GEN/G94/103/57/IMG/G9410357.pdf?OpenElement).

UN Working Group on Enforced or Involuntary Disappearances
- (1994). E/CN.4/1994/26.
- (1999. Visit to Sri Lanka 25-29 October 1999. E/CN.4/2000/64 Add.1 (http://daccessdds.un.org/doc/UNDOC/GEN/G99/164/79/PDF/G9916479.pdf?OpenElement).
- (2000). 18 December. E/CN.4/2001/68.
- (2008). Report to the Human Rights Council, A/HRC/7/2 (http://daccessdds.un.org/doc/UNDOC/GEN/G08/101/05/PDF/G0810105.pdf?OpenElement).

UNICEF
- (2006a). Children are victims of conflict in Sri Lanka, press release, 15 August (www.unicef.org).
- (2006b). Food supplies running low in Jaffna, 24 October (www.unicef.org/srilanka).
- (2006c). Sri Lankan schoolgirls killed and injured amid escalating violence, 16 August (www.unicef.org/infobycountry/sri_lanka_35357.html).
- (2008). Humanitarian Action Report: Sri Lanka (www.unicef.org/har08/index_sri_lanka.php).

US Committee for Refugees (1996). The people in between: Sri Lankan face long-term displacement as conflict escalates, March.

US Congress (2007), Foreign Operations, and Related Programs Appropriations Act, 2008 (Engrossed Amendment as Agreed to by Senate) for the fiscal year ending September 30, 2008, Sec 690, H.R.2764, Department of State (www.house.gov).

US State Department
- (2000) Sri Lanka: Country report on human rights practices 1999 (www.state.gov).
- (2001) Sri Lanka: Country report on human rights practices 2000   2001 (www.state.gov/countries).
- (2007). Mine Action Support Group Newsletter, First Quarter (www.state.gov).

Van Brabant K (1997). The Coordination of Humanitarian Action: the Case of Sri Lanka, RRN Network Paper 23 (http://repository.forcedmigration.org/show_metadata.jsp?pid–fmo:3629).

Vije M
- (1986). Militarization in Sri Lanka, Tamil Information Centre, London.
- (1993). Sri Lanka: Economic blockade, Tamil Information Centre, London.
- (2004). Situation in Sri Lanka, Swiss Refugee Council.

Watch List on Children and Armed Conflict (2008). No Safety No Escape: Children and the escalating armed conflict in Sri Lanka (www.watchlist.org).

Whitehall J (2007). Teaching Tamil Tigers, Medical Journal of Australia, 187, 11-12.

Whitehall J et al (2007). Snakebites in North-East Sri Lanka, International Electronic Journal of Rural and Remote Health Research, 12 December (www.rrh.org.au).

World Bank (2004). Sri Lanka: North-East housing reconstruction programme, Project Information Document (www.wds.worldbank.org/external/default/WDSContentServer/).

World Food Programme
- (2001). Nutritional survey of welfare centres in Jaffna District, Sivarajah N.
- (2007a). Sri Lanka Food Security Assessment Final report 15-30 April (http://documents.wfp.org/stellent/groups/public/documents/ena/wfp135041.pdf).
- (2007b). Sri Lanka - Integrated Food Security and Humanitarian Phase Classification (IPC), May (www.ipcinfo.org).

World Health Organization
- (2002). Health system and health needs of the North-East Sri Lanka, WHO Colombo.
- (2003). Sri Lanka: technical advice. Country visit undertaken for the purpose of mental health needs assessment in North-East Sri Lanka, June (www.who.int/mental health/policy).
- (2006). WHO country cooperation strategy 2006-2011: Democratic Socialist Republic of Sri Lanka, September 2006 (http://www.who.int/countryfocus/cooperation strategy/ccs_lka_en.pdf).

WHO and Office of the UN High Commissioner for Human Rights (2008). The Right to Health. Fact Sheet 31 (www.ohchr.org/Documents/Publications/Factsheet31.pdf).

9 781852 010218